The
Interdependence
Handbook

The Interdependence Handbook

Looking Back, Living the Present, Choosing the Future

Edited by
Sondra Myers and Benjamin R. Barber

International Debate Education Association
New York • Amsterdam • Brussels

Published in 2004 by
The International Debate Education Association
400 West 59th Street
New York, NY 10019

© 2004 by International Debate Education Association

Printed in the United States of America.

Sondra Myers and Benjamin R. Barber, Editors
Anu Yadav, Production Editor
Joshua Karant, Interdependence Index Editor

Design by Kathleen Hayes

Photo credits: pp. vii, ix, 19, 20, 23, 25, 62, 63—Andrei Jackamets;
14—Sergey Bermeniev (UN/DPI Photo); 16—courtesy Focolare Movement;
26—Leandre Jackson; 34—courtesy John F. Kennedy Library and Museum;
42—courtesy Office of William Jefferson Clinton; 53—Jerry Bauer;
56—J. Gardner; 59—Tsar Fedorsky; 66—Susanna Klassel.

Library of Congress Cataloging-in-Publication Data

The interdependence handbook: looking back, living the present, choosing
the future / edited by Sondra Myers and Benjamin R. Barber.
        p. cm.
        ISBN 1-932716-01-7 (alk. paper)
    1. International cooperation. 2. Globalization. 3. Social
participation. 4. Civics. I. Myers, Sondra.
        JZ1318I557 2004
        303.48'2—dc22
                                2004016532

Table of Contents

Introduction

Interdependence—what's that? That is the question *we* are asking here. Independence is much more familiar, as in the Declaration of Independence, which announced the establishing of a new American nation liberated from English rule. But interdependence is something else: it smacks a little of world government and the end of independent nation-states—an old-fashioned internationalism that people used to call, at best, unrealistic, and at worst, utopian or foolish.

But interdependence, as we try to understand it in this first decade of the 21st century, isn't a theory about how things should be or might be. It is a description of the way things have actually become. It doesn't say nations *ought* to think beyond their own borders, or that it would be *good* for them to be more dependent on one another. It says borders no longer mean very much, and that people and countries already *are* dependent on one another, whether they like it or not. And further, that if nations don't start thinking that way, we are not going to be able to deal with such devastating challenges as AIDS, drugs, illegal immigration, disappearing jobs, global markets, terrorism or, for that matter, much of anything else.

There was a time not so long ago when if you lived in Iowa or Florida or even New York or California, you could pretty well think about nothing but America, where the goods we made and consumed and the values we believed in and the aims and purposes we had were all "made in America." No more.

Most countries started realizing quite a while ago that they were not alone in the world and could not control their own destinies. Small countries like Poland and Costa Rica and Belgium have always known it; they knew they were dependent on what went on outside their own fragile frontiers. And by the end of World War II even larger countries in Europe that had enjoyed independence, figured out that going it alone had left them with hundreds of years of religious persecution, trade battles and territorial wars. That's when Germany and France and Italy and their neighbors began to talk less about sovereignty and their own rights, and more about Europe and their responsibilities to one another.

However, in the United States, with two great oceans separating it from the rest of the world, and with a bounteous continent that makes it feel self-sufficient, it's been harder to grasp the idea that it is dependent on faraway neighbors in everyday life. The truth is that there is almost nothing in life that doesn't depend, one way or the other, on people someplace else. That goes for the things we like, such as entertainment, electronics, clothes and food, and even knowledge and telephone service—and the things we fear, including global warming, diseases, drugs, crime and terrorism.

In other words, interdependence is a fact, pure and simple. And if that's so, then maybe the time has come to begin to think more seriously about how to deal with it. Because if all our ideas about democracy and citizenship and power and accountability are still confined inside a "box" called independence, tucked safely inside something called "the sovereign nation-state," we are not very likely to be able to address the harsh facts of interdependence that condition our reality.

Look at it this way: If we have diseases without borders but no health systems without borders, we are going to get sicker and sicker even as medicine gets better and better. If we have technology without borders, but no regulations without borders, how can we ensure that our information and entertainment systems are honest, truthful and free? If we have capitalism and markets and money and jobs without borders, but a government bound by borders, how can it preserve our economic security? Keep jobs at home? Keep unfair global competition at bay? Stop unfair trade and environmental and labor practices at home and elsewhere in the world? If we have crime without borders, don't we need police without borders? If we have conflicts and terrorism and wars without borders, surely we need politics and democracy and law without borders to deal with them. And now that we've become consumers without borders, we have to figure out how to become citizens without borders.

In short, once we become aware of what interdependence means, and how many kinds of destructive interdependence we may be facing, it will be easier for us to figure out how to think and act interdependently to deal with all the problems that interdependence brings—and work together to build a safer and more just future.

Interdependence is not a theory or an ideal, it's our reality. The question is "Can we make it democratic?"

Benjamin R. Barber
June 7, 2004

About The Interdependence Handbook

Can we change the way we think and act? Can we introduce a new guiding principle for civic behavior into our own minds and the minds of citizens throughout the world? *The Interdependence Handbook* is our affirmative answer to these questions. Because of the urgency of the need to find new approaches to solving old and new problems, approaches based on the realities of interdependence, we have gathered in one volume readings that focus on the "interdependence imperative." We have chosen works which portray the many aspects of interdependence that affect our daily lives—that give readers a three-dimensional picture of interdependence, in order to provide a solid foundation for thinking and acting interdependently in our very interconnected 21st century world.

The goals of the *Handbook* are, above all, civic. We must expand our view of civic responsibility to include all the world's people. We must come to understand that our actions in every realm—social, political, legal, environmental, religious and cultural— affect others; that we do not operate in a vacuum; that vacuums do not sustain life. We must learn about tolerance. We must appreciate diversity as the fertile and promising reality that it is, and act always as citizens of the world—knowing that the decisions that we make for ourselves will have an impact on others as well. And we must learn intolerance, too, and understand that it is neither ethical nor practical to tolerate a world divided between rich and poor, overfed and undernourished, healthy and diseased, educated and illiterate.

While it may be overwhelming to think of the vastness of the task that lies ahead, it gives comfort to know that we share responsibility for the future with all the world's people. Those of us who are fortunate enough to enjoy a fair measure of life and liberty must form a vanguard of informed, engaged citizens, willing to live and act according to the realities of interdependence.

We human beings have a great capacity to adapt to reality; we have exhibited it again and again through history. In the case of interdependence and its civic implications, we must ask ourselves, "Do we have the will to change?" I think we do, and offer *The Interdependence Handbook* as a guide to these changes.

Part One of *The Handbook* contains reflections from the first annual Interdependence Day, launched at the American Philosophical Society in Philadelphia on September 12, 2003. The program there was "From Independence to Interdependence—On the Continuum." These thoughtful remarks help clarify the meaning of interdependence and inspire us to adopt the interdependent worldview.

In Part Two we turn to "The Interdependence of Everything," excerpts from speeches by John F. Kennedy, Martin Luther King Jr. and Kofi Annan and essays by distinguished thinkers that look at interdependence as it pertains not only to political and civic life, but to religion, science and technology, and culture. Here we expand our understanding of the ubiquity of interdependence—of interdependence as an essential characteristic of virtually all the elements and institutions of the world we live in. Part Two also includes "Young Voices," a section that reflects the thinking of high school and college students—the generation that will, in the not-too-distant future, assume leadership.

Part Three, "Celebrating Interdependence Day—Every Year, Everywhere" is a practical guide to planning and conducting Interdependence Day as a very special commemorative occasion in schools, colleges, civic and cultural organizations and religious institutions and whole communities—this year and every year. It contains templates, "how-to" models for conducting Interdependence Day in your community. The templates will no doubt set you thinking creatively about ways to make Interdependence Day an important occasion in your own institution.

In addition you will find an index of fascinating facts about interdependence in Part Three, to give you some ideas about the many ways it crops up in our lives—for better and for worse.

Part Four contains documents of historical significance. These reflect the many efforts made over time by visionaries and realists to strengthen the ties among human beings and build a global community firmly grounded in the realities of interdependence.

The launch of Interdependence Day in Philadelphia in 2003 was a bold first step. Now the challenge is to give interdependence permanent status in our vocabularies and our actions, and to create a commemorative occasion that will serve as an enduring symbol of our commitment to a more sane and humane future. We want it to have the same important impact on the interdependence movement that Earth Day has had on the environmental movement. With your help, we will have the power to do that!

Sondra Myers
June 1, 2004

Part One

Reflections from the First Annual Interdependence Day
September 12, 2004

The launch of the first annual Interdependence Day in Philadelphia on September 12, 2003 in many ways set the standard for thinking about interdependence—and thinking interdependently. Greetings arrived from world leaders who were invited but could not attend the event, the Declaration of Interdependence was read by an intergenerational group, a choral work by renowned composer, John Duffy, The Interdependence Chorale, *was performed by the Philadelphia Singers, and thought-provoking and inspiring remarks were delivered by a number of distinguished speakers from a variety of perspectives. As you read the messages and the remarks, imagine hearing the noble music, the resounding power of the Declaration, and the electric rhythms of Sonia Sanchez' poem,* Peace. *And imagine a world in which people acknowledge interdependence as a reality, and expand their idea of civic responsibility to include all the world's people.*

☾

Discussion Questions

1. Interdependence Day calls to the mind of Václav Havel, Charter 77, the Czech human rights movement, which was based on two principles, solidarity and individual responsibility. Can you explain why?

2. Do you agree with Chiara Lubich that brotherhood is an essential element in "the political plan for humanity?"

3. Benjamin Barber sites the negative aspects of interdependence. Give two examples. What can "civic interdependence" do to reduce the impact of the negative forces? Give two examples.

4. Gary Hart says America has the choice of becoming an empire or remaining a republic? Which choice do you think it will make? Why?

5. According to Harry Belafonte, "we have come to realize that in . . . differences, and in our interdependence, lie the key to our humanity." Do you agree with him? Why or why not?

6. John Brademas cites several policies and practices that foster intermational cooperation. Can you cite ways that the Internet might be used in this regard?

7. What do the Sicilian Mafia, Osama bin Laden, and Adolf Hitler have in common, according to Leoluca Orlando?

8. In what way was Dr. King a "man for all seasons?"

9. What does Sonia Sanchez mean when she says, in her poem, *Peace*, that "a terrorist's bomb is the language of the unheard?"

Readings

Message from Kofi Annan
Secretary-General of the United Nations
Delivered by Edward Mortimer
Director of Communications, Secretary-General's office

The Declaration of Independence in Philadelphia in 1776 was part of a process, spread over many centuries and many lands, through which the world's peoples achieved self-government in independent states. That epoch continues into our own day. It was only last year, after all, that the people of Timor Leste achieved full national sovereignty, and joined the United Nations. Nevertheless, a new era is upon us. In the future, the map of the world may not change so much, but the world will be transformed in other ways—by the forces of globalization, and the growing interdependence of the world's peoples. In the era of independence, peoples have achieved and practice self-government within the framework of nation states. That framework is still very important, and will remain so even in the new era of interdependence. But the more interdependent we become, the more decisions have to be taken, not by one nation state alone, but by many, acting together. Unless it is properly managed, this process can entail a "democratic deficit," as decision-makers are further removed from and less accountable to the people whose lives are affected. So the challenge for all of us is to manage our interdependence in ways that bring people in, rather than shutting them out. Citizens need to think and act globally, so as to influence global decisions. And that means that the United Nations, in order to play its part, must live up to the first words of its Charter, "WE THE PEOPLES." I know it is in that spirit that you have gathered today in Philadelphia to declare your interdependence. I am sorry I cannot be with you in person, but I congratulate you, and wish you every success.

Message from Václav Havel
Former President of the Czech Republic
Delivered by Martin Palouš
Czech Ambassador to the United States

The idea to promulgate the Declaration of Interdependence the day after the anniversary of the horrible events of September 11, 2001, in the city where the American Constitution was born two hundred and seventeen years ago, is charged with lucid and compelling symbolism. The founding of the United States was one of the most important events in the beginning of the modern "enlightened" era—a bold decision of its founding fathers to enter into a social contract and to create a political body whose essence was respect for unalienable human rights, political liberties and social justice, the rule of law and the republican form of government.

Terrorism—whether fed by fundamentalist religious visions or mere lust for power—represents the most dangerous phenomenon at this moment in history. The United States is undoubtedly playing a crucial role in the struggle against its threat; still, the United States cannot do it alone. Do we need in the 21st century—in order to protect and preserve the values that once ignited the American Revolution—a new social contract, an agreement among all freedom-loving peoples on the earth, a new political principle that Hannah Arendt called for in her *Origins of Totalitarianism?*

I realize how complex the current political problems are, and how challenging it is to cope with all the questions we have to deal with today in our political thought. I wish your assembly success in laying the foundation for a new, important, genuinely post-modern political movement, and a new political tradition. I hope it can start a new open-minded, tolerant and creative dialogue concerning our global situation, and build gradually new transnational networks of commitment to the public interest and the common good.

Your efforts in Philadelphia remind me of the atmosphere of Charter 77, the Czechoslovak human rights movement of the 1970s and 1980s. It was based on two simple principles, vital for Charter 77's ability to survive as a kind of "parallel polis:" the principle of individual responsibility and the principle of solidarity.

On the one hand, everybody had to make up his or her mind alone and resist all sorts of doubts and pressures in order to sign the charter documents and participate in charter activities. On the other hand, Charter 77 could not have survived without the spirit of solidarity among its members, who often differed both in their past experience and current political opinions. Living together in one and the same situation, they were united by their common concern for human rights and the desire for human freedom and authenticity.

Let us hope that, in spite of all current challenges and threats, the word "interdependence" will always mean for us what it meant for the Polish workers in the shipyard in Gdansk in 1980, when they started to make their way from serfdom to freedom: an appeal to liberate ourselves from our fears and petty idiosyncratic concerns, an appeal to live like citizens of the world, true cosmopolitans, aware of our common responsibility and solidarity.

Message from Chiara Lubich
President of Focolare
Delivered by William Neu
Head of Focolare activities in North America

After September 11th, many of us wanted to work for a valid alternative to terrorism and war. Personally, I relived the devastation and feeling of powerlessness we experienced in the Italian city of Trent when it was bombed during World War II. Yet it was right beneath the bombs that our first companions and I discovered in the Gospel the light of mutual love, leading us to give our lives for one another. Convinced that love wins everything, even in the midst of that destruction, we wanted to share this love with all our neighbors, without discriminating among persons, groups, or peoples; without paying attention to social status, culture, or religious convictions.

Likewise, many of us are asking today, in New York as in Bogota, in Rome as in Nairobi, in London as in Baghdad, if it is possible to live in a world of peoples who are free, equal and united, not only respecting one another's identity, but also attentive to their particular needs.

There is only one answer: not only is it possible, but it is the very essence of the political plan for humanity.

Liberty and equality don't suffice in the face of present and future challenges. A third element, long forgotten in political thought and practice is needed: brotherhood. Without brotherhood, no person is actually free and equal. Equality and liberty will always be incomplete and precarious without fraternity in political processes. Brotherhood can give new meaning today to the reality of interdependence. Brotherhood can stimulate initiatives and recognize the complexities of our world. Brotherhood brings peoples out of isolation and offers development to those who are excluded. Brotherhood shows the way to resolving differences peacefully. Brotherhood allows us to dream and hope for a communion of goods among rich and poor countries, since the world's scandalous inequity is one of terrorism's main causes. Doesn't the name Philadelphia encourage brotherly love? Such brotherhood is the Focolare movement's sixty-year experience all over the world.

I hope this first Interdependence Day will be an opportunity to renew our commitment to work together for the unity of the whole human family, helping one another with dedication and trust.

From Independence to Interdependence
Benjamin R. Barber

Two hundred and twenty-seven years ago, in the belief that liberty and the autonomy of the sovereign state went hand in hand, America proclaimed its independence, or at least a group of white American property-owning males declared their independence from the colony that they had been part of, and from the British Empire. And for two centuries, America has pursued the sovereign ideal on the premise that the rights and social justice in whose name it has striven to become both democratic and free is the condition for liberty; that anyone who wants to be free must be independent. Indeed, those who were left out of the early republic fought in the name of their own independence from servitude to join and become part of the American nation and the world of the free.

Speaking not just for itself but for other nations as well, America has insisted that democracy is premised on national liberation, and that personal liberty requires national independence. A little less than fifteen years ago, peoples in Prague, Warsaw, and Moscow all reasserted the powerful connection between liberty and independence by declaring their own liberation from the domination of Soviet communism, reclaiming their liberty by asserting their right to be self-governing. And today, in parts of the world as different as Afghanistan, Liberia, Kosovo, and Brazil, nations continue to reassert their sovereign independence from domestic tyranny and foreign imperialism as the condition for the liberty of their people.

And yet nations that have long cherished their independence, as well as those that have recently struggled to achieve it, are learning the hard way that there is neither freedom, nor equality, nor safety from tyranny, nor security from terror, on the basis of independence alone. We are learning that in a world in which ecology, public health, markets, technology, and war affect everyone equally, interdependence is not an aspiration but a stark reality, upon which the survival of the human race depends. We are learning that where fear rules and terrorism is met merely by shock or awe, neither peace nor democracy can ensue; that while we have yet to construct those global institutions that might offer us a benevolent interdependence, we are beset by global entities that impose on us the costs of a malevolent and often anarchic interdependence. We are learning that in the absence of a new journey to democratize interdependence, we may lose the blessings conferred on us by the old journey to democratic independence. Where once nations depended on sovereignty alone to secure their destinies, today they depend on one another. In a world where the poverty of some imperils the wealth of others, none are safer than the least safe. Multilateralism is not a strategy of idealists, but a realistic necessity.

The lesson of 9/11 was not that rogue states could unilaterally be pre-empted and vanquished by a sovereign United States, but that sovereignty itself was becoming a

> Multilateralism is not a strategy of idealists, but a realistic necessity.
>
> —*Benjamin R. Barber*

chimera: HIV, global warming, predatory capital, nuclear proliferation, and transnational crime had stolen from America and other nations the substance of their cherished sovereignty well before the terrorists displayed their murderous contempt for it on that fateful morning just two years ago, in New York and Washington. America still seems to play the "Lone Ranger" in a world where, in truth, only global posses have a chance of succeeding. For interdependence is now our reality, and the acknowledgement of interdependence that we manifest and celebrate today is the necessary starting point for prudent foreign policy in America and for every nation in the world.

But we citizens do not have to await a president or a government to embrace interdependence. We can do it with them or without them. It is we who must start the work of constructing a civic architecture for global cooperation, as citizens, as NGOs, as members of global civil society. Interdependence Day and the Declaration of Interdependence, whose promulgation it marks, allow us to affirm the creative potential of what is now merely a grim reality. The simple fact is that no American child will ever again sleep safe in her bed if children in Baghdad, or Karachi, or Nairobi are not secure in theirs. Americans will not be permitted to feel proud of liberty if people elsewhere feel humiliated by servitude. This is not because America is responsible for everything that has happened to others, but because in a world of interdependence, the consequences of misery and injustice for some will be suffered by all.

On this September 12th, the journey from independence to interdependence—already a reality in terms of global anarchy—begins for us gathering in Philadelphia, and in Budapest, and in other places around this country and the world. Pledging ourselves citizens of one CivWorld—civic, civil, and civilized—recognizing our responsibilities to the common goods and liberties of humankind as a whole, we are pioneers on a journey in which every citizen—postman and president alike—must, in time, embark. Yesterday, we spent time remembering the dead; today we celebrate the living so that tomorrow we can embrace those who are not yet born. Harsh, malevolent interdependence has made us its servants. We now must make interdependence serve us by democratizing it, by embracing it, by creating a global architecture around it. With our friends in Budapest, we say, "Eoyotteles Napja;" next year in Rome, we will say with Mayor Veltroni, "Interdipendenza." To our allies in Germany, we say, "Zusammen lebren;" and to our friends in France, "L' Interdependence." Let this first Interdependence Day signal a beginning as promising for liberty and justice worldwide as July 4, 1776 was a beacon of light and promise for a handful of white property owners in America.

> It is we who must start the work of constructing a civic architecture for global cooperation, as citizens, as NGOs, as members of global civil society.
>
> —*Benjamin R. Barber*

Republic or Empire?

Gary Hart

It is entirely appropriate that we are gathered here today because, for the first time since the end of the Cold War, and the first time since we have entered a new century and millennium, the United States has begun a debate over what our role in the world should be. That debate began some months ago, without being announced as such. But the lines are being drawn as to whether, in the 21st century, the third century of its existence, this country will become an empire, or whether it will remain a republic. That is the huge issue that this nation is beginning to confront; and that is why an occasion such as this is so important.

Of the many reasons why this nation must resist the temptations of empire, I would like to cite only two. The first is that we're living in an age of profound multiple revolutions—revolutions that the imperial status of the United States would only turn toward the worse, and not toward the better. Globalization is one of them and the information revolution is another. Each by itself is historic and epic, but together they are transforming the world; and in many ways, for the better. They are bringing people together in terms of communication; they are breaking down barriers to trade and commerce and exchange. But they are also deepening the divide between the haves and the have-nots. Those nations that can benefit from trade and have access to the new technologies are doing better, while the two-thirds or more of the world that cannot participate in trade, and who do not have access to the digital technologies, are falling further behind.

Those two revolutions are leading to a third—the revolution in the status of the nation-state and the issue of sovereignty. It will be the big political issue of the 21st century. Either we will go it alone, or we will see that we are all in this together. And to be in this together leads inevitably to what I would call collaborative sovereignty—nations voluntarily surrendering part of their national sovereignty for the greater global good, in order to take advantage of globalization and the information revolution, and to stabilize the nations of the world, and expand them.

The erosion of nation-state sovereignty is leading to the fourth revolution, which we experienced profoundly in this nation two years ago this week, and that is the changing nature of conflict and warfare. If America seeks to be an empire and go it alone, we will be on our own in fighting this new form of conflict, and we will not succeed. We can only succeed as a family of nations. The second major reason why we must resist the imperial seduction is the nature of this nation. We are a republic—the people that founded this nation did not talk in the language democracy; they talked about forming a republic. Benjamin Franklin, when asked what was going on inside the Constitutional Convention, said, "We are creating a republic, if you can keep it." That is the profound challenge for America in the 21st century. A

> If America seeks to be an empire and go it alone, we will be on our own in fighting this new form of conflict, and we will not succeed. We can only succeed as a family of nations.
>
> —*Gary Hart*

republic is based on civic virtue and citizen duty; on popular sovereignty and not the sovereignty of the powerful; and on resistance to corruption and a sense of the commonwealth. An empire is a form of corruption. Nations are no longer commonwealths; the people of the world are the commonwealth. And it is the common good that we are here today to celebrate. America must resist the temptations of empire and strengthen and restore America as a republic.

Create a World Full of Greenery ...
Harry Belafonte

Interdependence is not an uncommon idea; we live our lives interdependently. From the social perspective, much of what I have sought to be and to do has been deeply rooted in the concept of interdependence.

There was a great sense of interdependence among most Americans who struggled through unemployment, hunger, and disenfranchisement during the Depression. My parents were immigrants from the Caribbean. As people of color, they came here with the same hopes and aspirations as those who had come from Europe and other places, but they found that there was not a level playing field. Those of color who came were relegated to the least of opportunities, put a great strain on our belief in our fellow beings. The founding fathers created this nation and gave us a republic that was based upon independence. However, the democracy that we set out to build was rooted in a moment of great tyranny. Not only did we dispossess the indigenous peoples of this nation, but in order to build this empire, we depended on other people of color from Africa. So while the experiment of democracy was unfolding for some, others were living out a life of tremendous horror and tragedy. The issue of slavery was finally confronted when the nation erupted into the Civil War. The Civil War brought the promise of the future, but instead, we went into a century of segregation, once again defying the great harmony and the great humanity that our founders envisioned.

During World War II, hordes embraced fascism, racism, and Aryanism. The world's so-called democracies came together to confront these evils, but most of the countries calling themselves democracies found themselves dependent upon their colonial peoples. And America, even in the moment of great segregation, called upon citizens of color to become part of the struggle to make the world safe for democracy and a higher order of truth and coexistence. At the end of that war, when many of us came home feeling this was a new day and a new order, we discovered there was no generosity for citizens of color who had participated in the war, and many of us had to embark upon a new journey for our independence in the midst of the exercise of this democracy.

To our joy and good fortune, Dr. Martin Luther King, Jr. came forward, and in his "Kingian" way, brought America to the threshold of its greatest promise. He understood that the world was interdependent; that each nation was dependent upon the other, each citizen upon the other; and he preached that. The struggle against segregation started here in the United States, and then caught fire among others in the world; Nelson Mandela in South Africa is a good example.

And now, instead of finding a globe filled with harmony, we find a planet filled with violence and oppression. As we come to this exercise of interdependence, it is really the last frontier. If we do not come to understand our interdependence and to take it to a new place of moral and social conduct, and re-shape the way in which we do politics, I'm afraid that the wars that we experience each day will become more violent and we will turn to the use of nuclear weapons to solve our problems. Interdependence Day gives us a chance to reflect on the meaning of mutual respect and mutual responsibility.

Citizens in our world are dying of hunger, dying of poverty, and dying of disease. The situation is totally unacceptable. We must look to interdependence as a guide, alleviate conditions in our own society, and create a world filled with greenery, food, and culture, and a great love and respect for each other, regardless of differences. We will embrace those differences not only because we find in them new ways to live, but also because we have come to realize that in those differences, and in our interdependence, lie the key to our humanity.

> We must look to interdependence as a guide, alleviate conditions in our own society, and create a world filled with greenery, food, and culture, and a great love and respect for each other, regardless of differences.
>
> —*Harry Belafonte*

Policies For a More Politically and Culturally Interdependent World
John Brademas

My thesis today is straightforward. At a time when our world is freighted with conflict and turmoil, war, and the threat of war, it is crucial that we forge the structures and processes of peace and stability for the institutions of education and culture. While knowledge alone is not enough to overcome the problems that afflict our troubled planet, there are policies and actions that we, especially in the democratic world, can pursue that can contribute substantially to our capacity to transform the concept of interdependence among nations into a reality. Let me be specific.

- First, if we are to enhance the prospect of genuine global interdependence, we must invest substantially more than we have been in the study of cultures and peoples other than our own. This means encouraging more exchanges of students and faculty with other countries by expanding funding for such exchanges; in particular, for the Fulbright and Arts America programs, even as we call on corporations and foundations to increase their sponsorship of international scholarly and cultural programs. And we must also do better to support international education in our own countries. In my judgment, one of the reasons the United States has suffered so many setbacks in places like Vietnam, Iran, Central America, and now Iraq, has been ignorance—ignorance of the cultures, languages, and societies with which we have been engaged.

- Second, in 1975, I was the co-author in Congress, with Senator Claiborne Pell of Rhode Island, of the Art and Artifacts Indemnity Act, which enables museums in the United States to borrow art from museums abroad without having to pay expensive commercial insurance. Under this law, if any art is lost or damaged, the U.S. Government will pay the cost. In over a quarter of a century, with 713 exhibitions indemnified, American museums have saved nearly $160 million in insurance premiums, while our taxpayers had no net loss. We could not mount a major exhibition of art from abroad in the United States without the Indemnity Act. Accordingly, I would encourage other countries to adopt similar measures to increase knowledge and appreciation of the cultures of societies other than their own. For example, the European Union could create an indemnity program to facilitate loans of art among EU member states.

- Third, in a talk some time ago at the American Academy in Berlin, I called for "a new philanthropy for the new Europe." The culture of philanthropy is not nearly so rooted in other countries as in ours. But philanthropic contributions to institutions of culture, learning, and health have proved indispensable to their strength in the United States. And crucial to stimulating philanthropic giving in America are laws that provide deductions against taxes for such gifts. So I urge other countries to take a careful look at their tax laws with a view toward bolstering philanthropy.

- Fourth, at least a few major universities in Europe and elsewhere in the world should develop centers, or at least substantial academic courses, on the political system of the United States. The American Constitution is based on the separation of powers. That means that when it comes to the making of national policy, Congress, unlike the legislature in a parliamentary system, has great power. But with 100 senators and 435 members of the House of Representatives, and lacking the disciplined political parties common in Europe, the U.S. Congress is not easy to understand. That's why I am working to create at NYU a Center for the Study of Congress as a policy-making institution. We will bring to the university senators and congressmen, current and former, presidents, cabinet secretaries, legislative and executive branch officials, scholars, journalists, students, and parliamentarians from other countries, to discuss the processes by which Congress shapes national policy.

And since citizens and leaders of other countries are directly affected by policies of the American government, it is in their interest to learn more about how our political system works. There are a number of universities in Europe offer courses on American art and literature; I propose that they give more attention to our politics as well.

- Fifth, cultural and educational institutions in Europe and North America need to teach about Islam. Many Americans have never met a Muslim, and most are quite ignorant of the traditions of Islam. Accordingly, unless Muslims want Americans to think that Islam is represented solely by Osama Bin Laden, they must give more attention to teaching us the best in their religious faith, while those of us who are not Muslims have a similar obligation to listen and to learn.

In short, I propose, in view of the position of the United States in the world, that we invest, both politically and financially, in such activities. As President Carter once said in a letter to Congress, "Tell the world about our society and politics—in particular, our commitment to cultural diversity and individual liberty." And, said Mr. Carter, we need "to tell ourselves about the world, so as to enrich our own culture as well as to give us the understanding to deal effectively with problems among nations."

Legality and the Culture of Lawfulness
Leoluca Orlando

The history of the world is the history of human beings. It is the history of women and men agreeing to live as members of a community, a tribe, a village, a city, or a state; and it is the history of power, too; power transformed into legality. It is the history of building and imposing views in the tribe, the village, the city, and the state. The history of human beings and the history of power are found at every stage of history. The citizen is a member of a community, having rights and duties; he or she belongs to the community and is the most important element within it. The human being became the citizen and the power became legality as the result of the great revolutions and constitutions in the last decades of the 18th century. For over 200 years, revolutions and constitutions have chosen the state as the fundamental community, and the citizen as the fundamental member of it. Many communities tried to promote legality not only as respect for the law, but also to ensure that the law was democratically chosen by the citizens; thus legality became the culture of lawfulness.

Identity-based illegality, or identity-based criminality, used "satanic verses" to pervert the Sicilian values of honor, family and friendship, and to pervert the Catholic faith. The worst enemy of Sicilian culture is the Sicilian Mafia boss; just as the worst enemy of Islamic culture is Osama Bin Laden; and the worst enemy of German culture was Adolf Hitler.

The culture of lawfulness is the expression used by the United Nations to recommend the strategic choice to promote good government and prevent crime in the world. The culture of lawfulness is the respect for the law, not merely for law enforcement, but for law as the daily way of life.

Lawfulness is both joyful and convenient. It is what I and others try to explain in Latin American countries. Starting from my own experience, and from the experience of many other countries that were hit by identity-based illegality, I can say that law enforcement is necessary, but not sufficient. We need the culture of lawfulness. Law enforcement and the culture of lawfulness need to go at the same speed, just like the two wheels of a cart. If the two wheels do not move simultaneously, the cart doesn't go forward—it spins around.

Today, the defense of the state is no longer sufficient; the tools we have built and collected, together with the state, are no longer adequate. We are here today because we recognize the importance of what happened 200 years ago in Philadelphia, in Paris, and in many other American and European cities. And we are here, too, because we believe that it is time to go forward; that to be a citizen of a state is no longer sufficient. The building process of the European Union, for example, comes out of this insufficiency. The EU is a union of 500 million human beings with a common citizenship.

I know it is a difficult thing to consider when so many people live in states that have almost nothing in common with the democratic states that we know. But in the long run, it is important for those people living in states without democratic legality that we try to build a better future. The need for a new legality and a new culture of lawfulness is no longer connected to the independence of a state, but rather to the interdependence of humankind.

Our ancestors built the states; they had to fight to be independent and create democratic rules. But we do not have to fight to be interdependent; we *are* interdependent. Humankind is interdependent—socially, politically, economically, culturally, and religiously. We must promote a new culture of lawfulness in the context of interdependence. Legality and the culture of lawfulness in the future will respect human rights even more than the legislation of the state. If we democratic states accept such a challenge, we will be the protagonists of the future—of the right to a better future for all human beings.

> The need for a new legality and a new culture of lawfulness is no longer connected to the independence of a state, but rather to the interdependence of humankind.
>
> —*Leoluca Orlando*

Dr. King's Legacy
Michael Thurman

As we think about America and what America has meant to all of us, we can recall those literature classes where we first became aware of Ralph Waldo Emerson, and ultimately, the Emersonian spirit that shaped American culture. It was fifty to sixty years after the American Revolution that Emerson defined the American spirit—that of rugged individualism. It has propelled our economy, it has driven our politics, and, indeed, it has driven every facet of American life.

However, on September 11, 2001 that spirit, that foundation was greatly challenged, and we've been called upon to reflect on and reevaluate that independence, and look toward the spirit of interdependence. As we saw, thousands of people were ruthlessly killed on 9/11, and our lives have been changed forever. Even as we speak today, America is having to learn the painful lesson of working cooperatively with our neighbors. To take on the Iraqi freedom project without support from the international community, we know was unwise, and our nation is having to retrace its steps and solicit UN support.

As I reflect on the writings of Dr. King nearly 40 years ago, I am amazed that his message was tremendously on target, and that it continues to be both timeless and timely. In 1967, when Dr. King delivered a Christmas sermon at Ebenezer Baptist Church in Atlanta, Georgia, it was broadcast by the Canadian Broadcasting Corporation as the final lecture of its Massey Lecture Series. The sermon was entitled, *A Christmas Sermon on Peace*. In this sermon, we see how globally-conscious King was in 1967. As you will recall, globalization and the global economy did not become buzzwords in American business until the 1990s. Dr. King was well ahead of the curve. In the sermon, he sought to apply internationally the principles of non-violence which had proven effective in the fight for racial justice in this country, in a war in which he fought for the rights and freedom of African-Americans whose lives had been crushed by slavery and Jim Crow-ism. He sought to apply the principles of non-violence to all areas of human conflict on an international scale. As I read an excerpt from the sermon, think about the times in which we live today.

"Now, let me first suggest that if we are to have peace on earth, our loyalties must become ecumenical rather than sectional. Our loyalties must transcend our race, our tribe, our class, and our nation, and this means we must develop a world perspective. No individual can live alone, and as long as we try, the more we are going to have war in this world. Now the judgment of God is upon us, and we must either learn to live together as brothers, or we are all going to perish together as fools."

Dr. King's words possess a measure of timelessness and relevance that make them just as on target today as they were 36 years ago. As we view the hot spots around the world, such as the Middle East, Liberia, Afghanistan, Iraq, North Korea, the

Philippines, Colombia, and others, it boils down to a simple matter of learning how to get along like brothers and sisters in an ever-shrinking world. Communications systems and transportation systems have shortened the time it takes to circumnavigate the globe considerably, and we must learn to employ these new and powerful tools for the betterment of mankind, and not for its destruction. Just as Dr. King urged us to be concerned with human relations, I am sure that he would continue to push the world toward a concentration on matters of human rights that is equal to our focus on technological advancement. After all, the great Creator has only given us one world to inhabit. America has seen three great movements: the American Revolution, the Civil War, and the Civil Rights Movement. Now we stand on the threshold of yet another great movement—the Interdependence Movement. Will we take the lead? Let's hope so.

Peace
(a poem for Maxine Green)
by Sonia Sanchez

    1. Peace. What is it?
        Is it an animal? A bird? A plane?
        (dooodoo doodee bopbopbop)

    2. Is it a verb? A noun? An adjective?
        Circling our paragraphed lives?
        (dwoodop bophop dwowaa)

    3. Du Bois said: The cause of war
        is the preparation of war.
        Du Bois said: The cause of war
        Is the preparation of war.
        I say the cause of peace
        Must be the preparation of peace
        I say the cause of peace
        Must be te preparation of peace.
        (blaablablabaaa blueeeeee)

4. Shall I prepare a table of peace
    before you in the presence of mine enemies?
    Shall I prepare a table of peace
    Will you know how to eat at this table?
    (doodala doodala doodala la la la lay)

5. Where are the forks of peace?
    Where are the knives of peace?
    Where are the spoons of peace?
    Where are the eyes of peace?
    Where are the hands of peace?
    Where are the children of peace?
    (Peace. Peace. dum dum dee dum dum)

6. Is peace an action? A way of life?
    Is it a tension in our earth body?
    Is peace you and I seeing beyond
    Bombs and babies roasting on a country road?
    (bop bop bop bop bop bop bop bopooooooueeeeeee).

7. Peace must not be still we have to
    Take it on the road, marching against
    Pentagon doors lurking in obscenity.
    Peace must not find us on our knees
    While a country holds hostage
    The hearts and penises of the workers.
    (blup blup blup blueee blup blup bluppp)

8. Can you say peace? Can you resurrect peace?
    Can you house the language of peace?
    Can you write a sermon of peace?
    Can you populate the chords of peace?
    (dee dee dadum peace la la la lalum peace)

9. A long time ago someone said: I think therefore I am
   A long time ago someone said: I think therefore I am
   Now we say: preemptive strikes there we are
   Now we say: preemptive strikes there we are
   (boom boom boom ay ay ay ay boomay boomay)

10. Can you rise up at the sound of peace?
    Can you fingerprint the land with peace?
    Can you become a star reflecting peace?
    Can your tongues flush peace
    Until peace becomes the noise of the planet
    Until peace becomes the noise of the planet
    (peaceeEeeeeEeeeEeeeeEeeEeeeEeeEeeeEE)

11. I know as MLK knew that the universe
    Is curved ultimately toward justice and peace.
    I know as MLK knew that the universe
    Is curved ultimately toward justice and peace
    for "war is the sanction of failure"
    for "war is the sanction of failure"
    (da-da-da-da-da-da-dee da-da-dadee)

12. Martin said a riot is the language of the unheard
    And I say a terrorist's bomb is the language of the unheard
    How to make the unheard heard?
    Without blowing themselves and the world up?
    (booom booom boom booooomm BOOOOM)

13. Mos Def said: Speech is my hammer
    Bang my world into shape
    Now let it fall.
    I say peace is my hammer
    Bang my world into peace
    And let it fall on the eyes of the children.
    (frère jacques dooodoodoo frère jacques dooooo doooo
    dormez-vous vous vous vous ding ding ding ding dong ding)

14. Where are the forks of peace?
     Where are the knives of peace?
     Where are the spoons of peace?
     Where are the eyes of peace?
     Where are the hands of peace?
     Where are the children of peace?

15. Where are you—you—youuuuuu (click)
     Where are you you you you youuuu (click)
     You you where are you you
     Where you where are youuu (click)
     Click-click-you-youuu (click)

Part Two

The Interdependence of Everything

The readings in this section aim to paint a verbal picture of interdependence, to demonstrate that it is not a new idea, and to point us in the direction of taking civic action that is based on the realities of interdependence. Though the "interdependence of everything" is, indeed, a reality, the decisions that we make and the actions that we take as human beings do have an impact on those realities. As Thomas Hughes points out in his essay, "Technological Interdependence," "Technology is not value free. It expresses the values of its creators and users." It is we who make the decisions to use technology in certain ways, ways that can be civically responsible or irresponsible. The same is true of our values as we address matters of health, wealth and the environment. As individuals we have personal needs that may be self serving; but as citizens we are charged with a public responsibility. It is a privilege to be a citizen of a democracy instead of a subject or victim of a totalitarian or authoritarian regime. We cannot hang on to the rights we cherish as citizens of a democracy—old or new—unless we fulfill the public obligation that we have to society. And in the 21st century, we cannot limit our sphere of influence and responsibility to our local community or even to our nation. We must consider the whole world our domain of responsibility, because we now know that, as Benjamin Barber reminds us in his essay in Part One, ". . . no American child will ever again sleep safe in her bed if children in Baghdad, or Karachi, or Nairobi are not secure in theirs."

Discussion Questions

1. On July 4, 1962, in a speech at Independence Hall in Philadelphia, President John F. Kennedy reviewed the history of independence and saw interdependence as the wave of the future. According to Kennedy, "on this Day of Independence . . . the United States will be ready for a Declaration of Interdependence." What did Kennedy mean? Why did he focus on interdependence on Independence Day?

2. Martin Luther King, Jr., in a Christmas sermon in 1967, preached that ". . . if we are to have peace on earth, our loyalties must become ecumenical rather than sectional, . . . [they] must transcend our race, our tribe, our class, and our nation; and this means that we must develop a world perspective." Why did King put so much emphasis on global responsibility when his goal was civil rights for blacks in the US?

3. Kofi Annan and Patrice Brodeur discuss the similarity in basic values among the major religions of the world. Religion at times divides people. How can we use religious values as well as other diverse value systems to bring people together and not separate them from each other?

4. Looking to the future, Martha Nussbaum stresses the importance of a liberal education in an interdependent world, and the need, through the arts and the humanities, to cultivate "the narrative imagination . . . the ability to think what it might be like to be in the shoes of a person different from oneself. . . ." How important is this aspect of an education for interdependence, from your perspective?

5. Shirin Ebadi tells us that "The challenge facing us today is to think like dreamers but act in a pragmatic manner. And let us remember that many of humanity's accomplishments began with dreams." Do you agree with her? Can idealism and pragmatism work hand in hand?

6. Whare are Joseph Stiglitz's views on development?

7. Samantha Power, in her article on Hannah Arendt, finds our time, this post-Cold War, post Communist period, to be, much like Arendt's age, "suspended 'between a no-longer and a not-yet.'" But she calls us on us not to retreat into private domains but to be political—so that "our fate becomes our own." Yet many young people believe that their actions won't count. How can we overcome that lack of interest or belief in public actions?

8. How does high school student Lilly Deng use her experiences in China and the US to inform and inspire her public life?

9. Tariq Adwan, a Palestinian pre-med student studying in the US, aims to work "to make sure every person in the world gets equal healthcare." And he adds,

". . . not because I am a nice person but because it's their right—and it's my responsibility." What does it take to acquire a sense of responsibility, particularly for all the world's people? How important is education? Family values? Religious values? Peer pressure? Television?

Readings

Speeches

from Address at Independence Hall
John F. Kennedy
July 4, 1962

. . . It is a high honor for any citizen of our great Republic to speak at this Hall of Independence on this day of Independence. To speak as President of the United States to the Chief Executives of our 50 States is both an opportunity and an obligation. The necessity for comity between the National Government and the several States is an indelible lesson of our long history.

Because our system is designed to encourage both differences and dissent, because its checks and balances are designed to preserve the rights of the individual and the locality against preeminent central authority, you and I, Governors, recognize how dependent we both are, one upon the other, for the successful operation of our unique and happy form of government. Our system and our freedom permit the legislative to be pitted against the executive, the State against the Federal Government, the city against the countryside, party against party, interest against interest, all in competition or in contention with one with another. Our task—your task in the State House and my task in the White House—is to weave from all these tangled threads a fabric of law and progress. We are not permitted the luxury of irresolution. Others may confine themselves to debate, discussion, and that ultimate luxury—free advice. Our responsibility is one of decision—for to govern is to choose.

Thus, in a very real sense, you and I are the executors of the testament handed down by those who gathered in this historic hall 186 years ago today. For they gathered to affix their names to a document which was, above all else, a document not of rhetoric but of bold decision. It was, it is true, a document of protest—but protests had been made before. It set forth their grievances with eloquence—but such eloquence had been heard before. But what distinguished this paper from all the others was the final irrevocable decision that it took—to assert the independence of free States in place of colonies, and to commit to that goal their lives, their fortunes, and their sacred honor.

Today, 186 years later, that Declaration whose yellowing parchment and fading, almost illegible lines I saw in the past week in the National Archives in Washington is still a revolutionary document. To read it today is to hear a trumpet call. For that Declaration unleashed not merely a revolution against the British, but a revolution in human affairs. Its authors were highly conscious of its worldwide implications. And George Washington declared that liberty and self-government everywhere were, in his words, "finally staked on the experiment entrusted to the hands of the American people."

This prophecy has been borne out. For 186 years this doctrine of national independence has shaken the globe—and it remains the most powerful force anywhere in the world today. There are those struggling to eke out a bare existence in a barren land who have never heard of free enterprise, but who cherish the idea of independence. There are those who are grappling with overpowering problems of illiteracy and ill-health and who are ill-equipped to hold free elections. But they are determined to hold fast to their national independence. Even those unwilling or unable to take part in any struggle between East and West are strongly on the side of their own national independence.

If there is a single issue that divides the world today, it is independence—the independence of Berlin or Laos or Viet-Nam; the longing for independence behind the Iron Curtain; the peaceful transition to independence in those newly emerging areas whose troubles some hope to exploit.

The theory of independence is as old as man himself, and it was not invented in this hall. But it was in this hall that the theory became a practice; that the word went out to all, in Thomas Jefferson's phrase, that "the God who gave us life, gave us liberty at the same time." And today this Nation—conceived in revolution, nurtured in liberty, maturing in independence—has no intention of abdicating its leadership in that worldwide movement for independence to any nation or society committed to systematic human oppression.

As apt and applicable as the Declaration of Independence is today, we would do well to honor that other historic document drafted in this hall—the Constitution of the United States. For it stressed not independence but interdependence—not the individual liberty of one but the indivisible liberty of all.

In most of the old colonial world, the struggle for independence is coming to an end. Even in areas behind the Curtain, that which Jefferson called "the disease of liberty" still appears to be infectious. With the passing of ancient empires, today less than 2 percent of the world's population lives in territories officially termed "dependent." As this effort for independence, inspired by the American Declaration

As apt and applicable as the Declaration of Independence is today, we would do well to honor that other historic document drafted in this hall—the Constitution of the United States. For it stressed not independence but interdependence—not the individual liberty of one but the indivisible liberty of all.

—*John F. Kennedy*

...[T]he Atlantic partnership of which I speak would not look inward only, preoccupied with its own welfare and advancement. It must look outward to cooperate with all nations in meeting their common concern. It would serve as a nucleus for the eventual union of all free men—those who are now free and those who are vowing that some day they will be free.

—*John F. Kennedy*

of Independence, now approaches a successful close, a great new effort—for interdependence—is transforming the world about us. And the spirit of that new effort is the same spirit which gave birth to the American Constitution.

That spirit is today most clearly seen across the Atlantic Ocean. The nations of Western Europe, long divided by feuds far more bitter than any which existed among the 13 colonies, are today joining together, seeking, as our forefathers sought, to find freedom in diversity and in unity, strength.

The United States looks on this vast new enterprise with hope and admiration. We do not regard a strong and united Europe as a rival but as a partner. To aid its progress has been the basic object of our foreign policy for 17 years. We believe that a united Europe will be capable of playing a greater role in the common defense, of responding more generously to the needs of poorer nations, of joining with the United States and others in lowering trade barriers, resolving problems of commerce, commodities, and currency, and developing coordinated policies in all economic, political, and diplomatic areas. We see in such a Europe a partner with whom we can deal on a basis of full equality in all the great and burdensome tasks of building and defending a community of free nations.

It would be premature at this time to do more than indicate the high regard with which we view the formation of this partnership. The first order of business is for our European friends to go forward in forming the more perfect union which will someday make this partnership possible.

A great new edifice is not built overnight. It was 11 years from the Declaration of Independence to the writing of the Constitution. The construction of workable federal institutions required still another generation. The greatest works of our Nation's founders lay not in documents and in declarations, but in creative, determined action. The building of the new house of Europe has followed the same practical, purposeful course. Building the Atlantic partnership now will not be easily or cheaply finished.

But I will say here and now, on this Day of Independence, that the United States will be ready for a Declaration of Interdependence, that we will be prepared to discuss with a united Europe the ways and means of forming a concrete Atlantic partnership, a mutually beneficial partnership between the new union now emerging in Europe and the old American Union founded here 175 years ago.

All this will not be completed in a year, but let the world know it is our goal.

In urging the adoption of the United States Constitution, Alexander Hamilton told his fellow New Yorkers "to think continentally." Today Americans must learn to think intercontinentally.

Acting on our own, by ourselves, we cannot establish justice throughout the world; we cannot insure its domestic tranquility, or provide for its common defense, or promote its general welfare, or secure the blessings of liberty to ourselves and our posterity. But joined with other free nations, we can do all this and more. We can assist the developing nations to throw off the yoke of poverty. We can balance our worldwide trade and payments at the highest possible level of growth. We can mount a deterrent powerful enough to deter any aggression. And ultimately we can help to achieve a world of law and free choice, banishing the world of war and coercion.

For the Atlantic partnership of which I speak would not look inward only, preoccupied with its own welfare and advancement. It must look outward to cooperate with all nations in meeting their common concern. It would serve as a nucleus for the eventual union of all free men—those who are now free and those who are vowing that some day they will be free.

On Washington's birthday in 1861, standing right there, President-elect Abraham Lincoln spoke in this hall on his way to the Nation's Capital. And he paid a brief but eloquent tribute to the men who wrote, who fought for, and who died for the Declaration of Independence. Its essence, he said, was its promise not only of liberty "to the people of this country, but hope to the world . . . [hope] that in due time the weights should be lifted from the shoulders of all men, and that all should have an equal chance.

On this fourth day of July, 1962, we who are gathered at this same hall, entrusted with the fate and future of our States and Nation, declare now our vow to do our part to lift the weights from the shoulders of all, to join other men and nations in preserving both peace and freedom, and to regard any threat to the peace or freedom of one as a threat to the peace and freedom of all. "And for the support of this Declaration, with a firm reliance on the protection of Divine Providence, we mutually pledge to each other our Lives, our Fortunes and our sacred Honor."

From an address by President John Fitzgerald Kennedy delivered in Philadelphia July 4, 1962. Archived at the John F. Kennedy Library and Museum.

from Christmas Sermon on Peace
Martin Luther King, Jr.
December 24, 1967

Peace on Earth. . . . This Christmas season finds us a rather bewildered human race. We have neither peace within nor peace without. Everywhere paralyzing fears harrow people by day and haunt them by night. Our world is sick with war; everywhere we turn we see its ominous possibilities. And yet, my friends, the Christmas hope for peace and good will toward all men can no longer be dismissed as a kind of pious dream of some utopian. If we don't have good will toward men in this world, we will

We have experimented with the meaning of nonviolence in our struggle for racial justice in the United States, but now the time has come for man to experiment with nonviolence in all areas of human conflict, and that means nonviolence on an international scale.

—*Martin Luther King, Jr.*

destroy ourselves by the misuse of our own instruments and our own power. Wisdom born of experience should tell us that war is obsolete. There may have been a time when war served as a negative good by preventing the spread and growth of an evil force, but the very destructive power of modern weapons of warfare eliminates even the possibility that war may any longer serve as a negative good. And so, if we assume that life is worth living, if we assume that mankind has a right to survive, then we must find an alternative to war—and so let us this morning explore the conditions for peace. Let us this morning think anew on the meaning of that Christmas hope: "Peace on Earth, Good Will toward Men." And as we explore these conditions, I would like to suggest that modern man really go all out to study the meaning of nonviolence, its philosophy and its strategy.

We have experimented with the meaning of nonviolence in our struggle for racial justice in the United States, but now the time has come for man to experiment with nonviolence in all areas of human conflict, and that means nonviolence on an international scale.

Now let me suggest first that if we are to have peace on earth, our loyalties must become ecumenical rather than sectional. Our loyalties must transcend our race, our tribe, our class, and our nation; and this means we must develop a world perspective. No individual can live alone; no nation can live alone, and as long as we try, the more we are going to have war in this world. Now the judgment of God is upon us, and we must either learn to live together as brothers or we are all going to perish together as fools.

Yes, as nations and individuals, we are interdependent. I have spoken to you before of our visit to India some years ago. It was a marvelous experience; but I say to you this morning that there were those depressing moments. How can one avoid being depressed when one sees with one's own eyes evidences of millions of people going to bed hungry at night? How can one avoid being depressed when one sees with ones own eyes thousands of people sleeping on the sidewalks at night? More than a million people sleep on the sidewalks of Bombay every night; more than half a million sleep on the sidewalks of Calcutta every night. They have no houses to go into. They have no beds to sleep in. As I beheld these conditions, something within me cried out: "Can we in America stand idly by and not be concerned?" And an answer came: "Oh, no!" And I started thinking about the fact that right here in our country we spend millions of dollars every day to store surplus food; and I said to myself: "I know where we can store that food free of charge—in the wrinkled stomachs of the millions of God's children in Asia, Africa, Latin America, and even in our own nation, who go to bed hungry at night."

It really boils down to this: that all life is interrelated. We are all caught in an inescapable network of mutuality, tied into a single garment of destiny. Whatever affects one directly, affects all indirectly. We are made to live together because of the interrelated structure of reality. Did you ever stop to think that you can't leave for your job in the morning without being dependent on most of the world? You get up in the morning and go to the bathroom and reach over for the sponge, and that's handed to you by a Pacific islander. You reach for a bar of soap, and that's given to you at the hands of a Frenchman. And then you go into the kitchen to drink your coffee for the morning, and that's poured into your cup by a South American. And maybe you want tea: that's poured into your cup by a Chinese. Or maybe you're desirous of having cocoa for breakfast, and that's poured into your cup by a West African. And then you reach over for your toast, and that's given to you at the hands of an English-speaking farmer, not to mention the baker. And before you finish eating breakfast in the morning, you've depended on more than half of the world. This is the way our universe is structured, this is its interrelated quality. We aren't going to have peace on earth until we recognize this basic fact of the interrelated structure of all reality. . . .

Now let me say that the next thing we must be concerned about if we are to have peace on earth and good will toward men is the nonviolent affirmation of the sacredness of all human life. Every man is somebody because he is a child of God. And so when we say "Thou shalt not kill," we're really saying that human life is too sacred to be taken on the battlefields of the world. Man is more than a tiny vagary of whirling electrons or a wisp of smoke from a limitless smoldering. Man is a child of God, made in His image, and therefore must be respected as such. Until men see this everywhere, until nations see this everywhere, we will be fighting wars. One day somebody should remind us that, even though there may be political and ideological differences between us, the Vietnamese are our brothers, the Russians are our brothers, the Chinese are our brothers; and one day we've got to sit down together at the table of brotherhood.

. . . In 1963, on a sweltering August afternoon, we stood in Washington, D.C., and talked to the nation about many things. Toward the end of that afternoon, I tried to talk to the nation about a dream that I had had, and I must confess to you today that not long after talking about that dream I started seeing it turn into a nightmare. I remember the first time I saw that dream turn into a nightmare, just a few weeks after I had talked about it. It was when four beautiful, unoffending, innocent Negro girls were murdered in a church in Birmingham, Alabama. I watched that dream turn into a nightmare as I moved through the ghettos of the nation and saw my black brothers and sisters perishing on a lonely island of poverty in the midst of a vast ocean of material prosperity, and saw the nation doing nothing to grapple with the Negroes' problem of poverty. I saw that dream turn into a nightmare as I watched my black brothers and sisters in the midst of anger and understandable outrage, in the midst of their hurt, in the midst of their disappointment, turn to misguided riots to try to solve that problem. I saw that dream turn into a nightmare as I watched the war in

...[W]e must either learn to live together as brothers or we are all going to perish together as fools.... [A]s nations and individuals, we are interdependent.

—*Martin Luther King, Jr.*

Vietnam escalating, and as I saw so-called military advisors, sixteen thousand strong, turn into fighting soldiers until today over five hundred thousand American boys are fighting on Asian soil. Yes, I am personally the victim of deferred dreams, of blasted hopes, but in spite of that I close today by saying I still have a dream, because, you know, you can't give up in life. If you lose hope, somehow you lose that vitality that keeps life moving, you lose that courage to be, that quality that helps you go on in spite of all. And so today I still have a dream.

I have a dream that one day men will rise up and come to see that they are made to live together as brothers. I still have a dream this morning that one day every Negro in this country, every colored person in the world, will be judged on the basis of the content of his character rather than the color of his skin, and every man will respect the dignity and worth of human personality. I still have a dream that one day the idle industries of Appalachia will be revitalized, and the empty stomachs of Mississippi will be filled, and brotherhood will be more than a few words at the end of a prayer, but rather the first order of business on every legislative agenda. I still have a dream today that one day justice will roll down like water, and righteousness like a mighty stream. I still have a dream today that in all of our state houses and city halls men will be elected to go there who will do justly and love mercy and walk humbly with their God. I still have a dream today that one day war will come to an end, that men will beat their swords into plowshares and their spears into pruning hooks, that nations will no longer rise up against nations, neither will they study war any more. I still have a dream today that one day the lamb and the lion will lie down together and every man will sit under his own vine and fig tree and none shall be afraid. I still have a dream today that one day every valley shall be exalted and every mountain and hill will be made low, the rough places will be made smooth and the crooked places straight, and the glory of the Lord shall be revealed, and all flesh shall see it together. I still have a dream that with this faith we will be able to adjourn the councils of despair and bring new light into the dark chambers of pessimism. With this faith we will be able to speed up the day when there will be peace on earth and good will toward men. It will be a glorious day, the morning stars will sing together, and the sons of God will shout for joy.

> We are all caught in an inescapable network of mutuality, tied into a single garment of destiny. Whatever affects one directly, affects all indirectly. We are made to live together because of the interrelated structure of reality.
>
> —*Martin Luther King, Jr.*

Nobel Peace Prize Lecture
Kofi Annan
December 10, 2001

. . . The idea that there is one people in possession of the truth, one answer to the world's ills, or one solution to humanity's needs, has done untold harm throughout history—especially in the last century. Today, however, even amidst continuing ethnic conflict around the world, there is a growing understanding that human diversity is both the reality that makes dialogue necessary, and the very basis for that dialogue.

We understand, as never before, that each of us is fully worthy of the respect and dignity essential to our common humanity. We recognize that we are the products of many cultures, traditions and memories; that mutual respect allows us to study and learn from other cultures; and that we gain strength by combining the foreign with the familiar.

In every great faith and tradition one can find the values of tolerance and mutual understanding. The Qur'an, for example, tells us that "We created you from a single pair of male and female and made you into nations and tribes, that you may know each other." Confucius urged his followers: "when the good way prevails in the state, speak boldly and act boldly. When the state has lost the way, act boldly and speak softly." In the Jewish tradition, the injunction to "love thy neighbour as thyself," is considered to be the very essence of the Torah.

This thought is reflected in the Christian Gospel, which also teaches us to love our enemies and pray for those who wish to persecute us. Hindus are taught that "truth is one, the sages give it various names." And in the Buddhist tradition, individuals are urged to act with compassion in every facet of life.

Each of us has the right to take pride in our particular faith or heritage. But the notion that what is ours is necessarily in conflict with what is theirs is both false and dangerous. It has resulted in endless enmity and conflict, leading men to commit the greatest of crimes in the name of a higher power.

It need not be so. People of different religions and cultures live side by side in almost every part of the world, and most of us have overlapping identities which unite us with very different groups. We *can* love what we are, without hating what—and who—we are not. We can thrive in our own tradition, even as we learn from others, and come to respect their teachings.

This will not be possible, however, without freedom of religion, of expression, of assembly, and basic equality under the law. Indeed, the lesson of the past century has been that where the dignity of the individual has been trampled or threatened—where citizens have not enjoyed the basic right to choose their government, or the

. . . [E]ven amidst continuing ethnic conflict around the world, there is a growing understanding that human diversity is both the reality that makes dialogue necessary, and the very basis for that dialogue.

—*Kofi Annan*

People of different religions and cultures live side by side in almost every part of the world, and most of us have overlapping identities which unite us with very different groups. We *can* love what we are, without hating what—and who—we are not. We can thrive in our own tradition, even as we learn from others, and come to respect their teachings.

—*Kofi Annan*

right to change it regularly—conflict has too often followed, with innocent civilians paying the price, in lives cut short and communities destroyed.

The United Nations, whose membership comprises almost all the States in the world, is founded on the principle of the equal worth of every human being. It is the nearest thing we have to a representative institution that can address the interests of all states, and all peoples.

—*Kofi Annan*

The obstacles to democracy have little to do with culture or religion, and much more to do with the desire of those in power to maintain their position at any cost. This is neither a new phenomenon nor one confined to any particular part of the world. People of all cultures value their freedom of choice, and feel the need to have a say in decisions affecting their lives.

The United Nations, whose membership comprises almost all the States in the world, is founded on the principle of the equal worth of every human being. It is the nearest thing we have to a representative institution that can address the interests of all states, and all peoples. Through this universal, indispensable instrument of human progress, States can serve the interests of their citizens by recognizing common interests and pursuing them in unity. No doubt, that is why the Nobel Committee says that it "wishes, in its centenary year, to proclaim that the only negotiable route to global peace and cooperation goes by way of the United Nations".

I believe the Committee also recognized that this era of global challenges leaves no choice but cooperation at the global level. When States undermine the rule of law and violate the rights of their individual citizens, they become a menace not only to their own people, but also to their neighbours, and indeed the world. What we need today is better governance—legitimate, democratic governance that allows each individual to flourish, and each State to thrive.

From the Nobel Lecture given by the Nobel Peace Prize Laureate Kofi A. Annan in Oslo, Norway December 10, 2001. Copyright © The Nobel Foundation, Stockholm, 2001.

from the First Annual Dole Lecture at the University of Kansas
William Jefferson Clinton
May 21, 2004

. . . Arguably the most partisan time in American history in terms of personal attacks, before the last 10 years, was in the early republic. Go back and read what Thomas Jefferson and John Adams and their supporters said about each other. Those guys started this country off and quit talking for 20 years because they were so mean. Why? Because after George Washington left the scene, who knew what America meant? We didn't have a national economy. Were we going to build one? We didn't have a national legal system. Were we going to have one? And while the matter was in doubt, the partisanship raged.

So instead of moaning about this or throwing up your hands about this, let's get about the business at hand. How should we look at the 21st century world? How can we develop a consensus that we can then have a Republican and a Democratic response to that would be civilized and lead to positive, constructive, honorable compromise?

This is the best I can do. I believe we live in an age normally referred to as globalization, sometimes referred to as the global information society. I prefer the term "interdependence," because it goes far beyond economics. There's good and bad in it. I have a cousin that lives in the hills of northwest Arkansas that plays chess over the Internet with a guy in Australia twice a week. They take turns figuring out who's got to stay up late. On the other hand, 9/11 was a testimony to the power of interdependence. . . . The Al Qaida . . . used open borders, easy travel, easy access to information and technology to turn an airplane into a weapon of mass destruction, to murder nearly 3,100 people, in Washington, Pennsylvania and New York from 70 countries. It's a story of global interdependence; the dark side of global interdependence.

When I was President, 30% of the economic growth that we had came from trade. When I was President, Senator Dole was always pushing me until we got it right— to end the ethnic slaughter in Bosnia. A hundred years ago, we wouldn't have known how to find Bosnia on a map. But it offended us because we had to watch those people being killed just because they were Muslims, and because we wanted Europe to be united and peaceful and democratic for the first time in history, to make the Cold War all worthwhile. So then we would be united, we'd be working together, we'd be fighting the problems of the rest of the world together. That, too, is interdependence.

So if interdependence can be positive or negative, it's obvious what we ought to be doing. . . . We need a strategy that builds up the positive and beats down the negative. We need to recognize that interdependence is inherently an unstable condition, and we need to move the world toward a more integrated, global community defined by three things: shared benefits, shared responsibilities and shared values. That's what I believe. . .

So . . . how would you go about making a world with more friends and fewer enemies? First of all, you've got to realize that half the people that live on earth aren't part of this globalized economy that works. Half the people live on less than $2 a day; of the 6 billion people on earth, 1 billion live on less than $1 a day, a billion and a half people never get a clean glass of water, a billion people go to bed hungry every night, 10 million kids die of preventable childhood diseases, and one in four deaths every year on earth now come from AIDS, TB, malaria and infections related to diarrhea. Most of them are little children who never got a single clean glass of water in their lives. So for a tiny fraction of what we spend on defense and

...we live in an age normally referred to as globalization, sometimes referred to as the global information society. I prefer the term "interdependence," because it goes far beyond economics.

—*William Jefferson Clinton*

... if interdependence can be positive or negative, it's obvious what we ought to be doing.... We need a strategy that builds up the positive and beats down the negative. We need to recognize that interdependence is inherently an unstable condition, and we need to move the world toward a more integrated, global community defined by three things: shared benefits, shared responsibilities and shared values. That's what I believe...

—*William Jefferson Clinton*

homeland defense, and I do mean tiny, we could double what we spend to help put all the children in the world who aren't in school in school, to pay our fair share of the fight against the world's diseases—and to do these other things. And to give you an example, after 9/11, I think we increased defense and homeland defense 60 something billion dollars in one year. We could double our assistance programs in these other areas, for about $10 or $12 billion. In a budget that must now be nearly $2 trillion. . . . The third thing I think is to find more ways to cooperate institutionally. This is a big challenge for America because we're going through a period in history when we have unrivalled military, economic, and political power. So every time we make a deal with anybody to do anything, we're giving up some of our freedom of action. Maybe a good deal for them, not a good deal for us because most of the time we can do whatever we please. The problem is, we will not be the only military, economic, and political superpower forever. If present growth rates continue, China, India, and the European Union will equal or surpass the United States sometime in the 21st century, just because of their size. They may not ever have to reach the per capita income we do to have greater output. . . . It puts a whole different cast on the debates you hear today over putting up missile defense, getting rid of the antiballistic missile treaty, should we be part of the comprehensive treaty, should we be part of the criminal court, should we be part of the Kyoto Climate Change Accord. . . . I didn't join the land mine treaty because they wrote it in a way that was absolutely hostile to the United States, and we have the finest record of any country in the world in promoting demining in the last 15 years, and it had enormous bipartisan support. Bob supported it. I'm not saying we can join every treaty, but I'm saying we should have a preference for being part of every conceivable network that will bring people together, because . . . it builds the habit of working with other people. And the more you're in the habit of believing that if you stay on the team, good things will happen, as compared to if you get off the team, the more likely we are to find peace and resolution to the problems of the 21st century. . . . Fourth thing is, we have to keep making America better. A lot of our influence in the world comes not from the size of our military or our arsenal of weapons, but from the power of our example. One of the schools that was destroyed in New York City on September 11th, 2001, the children had to leave and meet in a temporary facility. So Hillary and I went to this school to see these kids. 600 kids from over 80 different national racial and ethnic groups. One school. If we can prove that freedom brings mutual respect and that people can be proud of their heritage and proud of their religion, and proud of everything that's special and still bound together in a more perfect union, that will do as much to undermine the long-term appeal of terror as anything else we can do. Just continuing to prove America works.

Excerpted from the first annual Robert J. Dole Lecture by William Jefferson Clinton at the University of Kansas May 21, 2004.

. . . [W]e should have a preference for being part of every conceivable network that will bring people together, because . . . it builds the habit of working with other people.

—*William Jefferson Clinton*

Islam, Democracy and Human Rights
Shirin Ebadi
May 12, 2004

Whether we like it or not, the general phenomenon of globalization has globalized war and peace. Without being involved in the war, you wake up one day and see that its consequences have engulfed you. As such, if we desire a peaceful world, we have to struggle for it, both in our own countries and elsewhere. We have to encourage the development of global perspectives and broaden our concern for peace and human rights beyond the borders of our own societies. You who live in America cannot remain indifferent to violations of human rights in Afghanistan, Iraq, in Palestine, Iran, or in other parts of the world. We are all on the same boat and we all sail toward a greater civilization. Any damage to any part of the vessel will disrupt or hinder its movement.

The fate of humanity is so intertwined that one can no longer consider the blessings of this world one's own and deprive others of them at the same time. Globalization would be a positive historical development only if it can increase the prospects for international peace and reduce poverty and inequality in the world. We need the kind of globalization that paves the way for the creation of a transnational and international check on the abuse of national power and exploitation of labor.

I sound like a dreamer, I know. I am a dreamer when, in the midst of the turmoil in the Islamic world, I dream and I imagine a dynamic Islam that not only is entirely compatible with democracy and human rights, but can be made to carry the banner of advancing these causes throughout the world. I am a dreamer when I see a globalized humanity of the heart where every human being feels the pain of the other as if it were his or her own. And yes, I am a dreamer when I think dreams are—have always been—a crucial part of human history. The challenge facing us today is to think like dreamers but act in a pragmatic manner. And let us remember that many of humanity's accomplishments began as dreams.

Excerpted from an address by the same title delivered at the University of Maryland May 12, 2004. Copyright © 2004 by Shirin Ebadi. Reprinted with permission of Shirin Ebadi.

Whether we like it or not, the general phenomenon of globalization has globalized war and peace. Without being involved in the war, you wake up one day and see that its consequences have engulfed you.

—Shirin Ebadi

The challenge facing us today is to think like dreamers but act in a pragmatic manner. And let us remember that many of humanity's accomplishments began as dreams.

—Shirin Ebadi

Essays and Articles

from *Globalization and its Discontents*
Joseph Stiglitz

. . . Today globalization is being challenged around the world. There is discontent with globalization, and rightfully so. Globalization can be a force for good: the globalization of ideas about democracy and of civil society have changed the way people think, while global political movements have led to debt relief and the treaty on land mines. Globalization has helped hundreds of millions of people attain higher standards of living, beyond what they, or most economists, thought imaginable but a short while ago. The globalization of the economy has benefited countries that took advantage of it by seeking new markets for their exports and by welcoming foreign investment. Even so, the countries that have benefited the most have been those that took charge of their own destiny and recognized the role government can play in development rather than relying on the notion of a self-regulated market that would fix its own problems.

But for millions of people globalization has not worked. Many have actually been made worse off, as they have seen their jobs destroyed and their lives become more insecure. They have felt increasingly powerless against forces beyond their control. They have seen their democracies undermined, their cultures eroded.

If globalization continues to be conducted in the way that it has been in the past, if we continue to fail to learn from our mistakes, globalization will not only not succeed in promoting development but will continue to create poverty and instability. Without reform, the backlash that has already started will mount and discontent with globalization will grow.

This will be a tragedy for all of us, and especially for the billions who might otherwise have benefited. While those in the developing world stand to lose the most economically, there will be broader political ramifications that will affect the developed world too. . . .

The current situation reminds me of the world some seventy years ago. As the world plummeted into the Great Depression, advocates of the free market said, "Not to worry; markets are self-regulating, and given time, economic prosperity will resume." Never mind the misery of those whose lives are destroyed waiting for this so-called eventuality. Keynes argued that markets were not self-correcting, or not at least in a relevant time frame. (As he famously put it, "In the long run, we are all dead.")[1] Unemployment could persist for years, and government intervention was required. Keynes was pilloried—attacked as a Socialist, a critic of the market. Yet

---

1 J.M. Keynes A Tract on Monetary Reform (London MacMillian, 1924).

in a sense, Keynes was intensely conservative. He had a fundamental belief in the markets: if only government could correct this one failure, the economy would be able to function reasonably efficiently. He did not want a wholesale replacement of the market system; but he knew that unless these fundamental problems were addressed, there would be enormous popular pressures. And Keynes's medicine worked: since World War II, countries like the United States, following Keynesian prescriptions, have had fewer and shorter-lived downturns, and longer expansions than previously.

Today, the system of capitalism is at a crossroads just as it was during the Great Depression . . .

Thankfully, there is a growing recognition of these problems and increasingly political will to do something . . .

It is clear that there must be a multipronged strategy of reform. One should be concerned with reform of the international economic arrangements. But such reform will be a long time coming. Thus, the second prong should be directed at encouraging reforms that each country can take upon itself. The developed countries have a special responsibility, for instance, to eliminate their trade barriers, to practice what they preach. But while the developed countries' responsibility may be great, their incentives are weak: after all, off-shore banking centers, and hedge funds serve interests in the developed countries, and the developed countries can withstand well the instability that a failure to reform might bring to the developing world. . . .

Hence, the developing countries must assume responsibility for their well-being themselves. They can manage their budgets so that they live within their means, meager though that might be, and eliminate the protectionist barriers which, while they may generate large profits for a few, force consumers to pay higher prices. They can put in place strong regulations to protect themselves from speculators from the outside or corporate misbehavior from the inside. Most important, developing countries need effective governments, with strong and independent judiciaries, democratic accountability, openness and transparency and freedom from the corruption that has stifled the effectiveness of the public sector and the growth of the private.

What they should ask of the international community is only this: the acceptance of their need, and right, to make their own choices, in ways which reflect their own political judgments about who, for instance, should bear what risks. They should be encouraged to adopt bankruptcy laws and regulatory structures adapted to their own situations, not to accept templates designed by and for the more developed countries.

What is needed are policies for sustainable, equitable and democratic growth. This is the reason for development. Development is not about helping a few people get rich or creating a handful of pointless protected industries that only benefit the country's elite; it is not about bringing in Prada and Benetton, Ralph Lauren or Lou-

Development is about transforming societies, improving the lives of the poor, enabling everyone to have a chance at success and access to health care and education.... Developing countries must take charge of their own futures.

—*Joseph Stiglitz*

is Vuitton, for the urban rich and leaving the rural poor in their misery. Being able to buy Gucci handbags in Moscow department stores did not mean that country had become a market economy. Development is about transforming societies, improving the lives of the poor, enabling everyone to have a chance at success and access to health care and education.

This sort of development won't happen if only a few people dictate the policies a country must follow. Making sure that democratic decisions are made means ensuring that a broad range of economists, officials, and experts from developing countries are actively involved in the debate. It also means that there must be broad participation that goes well beyond the experts and politicians. Developing countries must take charge of their own futures. But we in the West cannot escape our responsibilities.

It's not easy to change how things are done. Bureaucracies, like people, fall into bad habits, and adapting to change can be painful. But the international institutions must undertake the perhaps painful changes that will enable them to play the role they should be playing to make globalization work, and work not just for the well off and the industrial countries, but for the poor and the developing nations.

The developed world needs to do its part to reform the international institutions that govern globalization. We set up these institutions and we need to work to fix them. If we are to address the legitimate concerns of those who have expressed a discontent with globalization, if we are to make globalization work for the billions of people for whom it has not, if we are to make globalization with a human face succeed, then our voices must be raised. We cannot, we should not, stand idly by.

. . . The events of the past year have brought home more forcefully than ever that we are interdependent—globalization is a fact of life. With interdependence comes a need for collective action, for people around the world to work together to solve the problems that we face, whether they be global risks to health, the environment, or economic or political stability. But democratic globalization means that these decisions must be made with the full participation of all the peoples of the world. Our system of global governance without global government can only work if there is an acceptance of a multilateralism. Unfortunately, the past year has seen an increase in unilateralism by the government of the world's richest and most powerful country. If globalization is to work, this too must change.

ᙦ

Why America Still Needs the United Nations

Shashi Tharoor

. . . When the [Iraq] crisis has passed, the world will still be left with, to use [Kofi] Annan's phrase, innumerable "problems without passports," threats such as the proliferation of weapons of mass destruction (WMD), the degradation of our common environment, contagious disease and chronic starvation, human rights and human wrongs, mass illiteracy and massive displacement. These are problems that no one country, however powerful, can solve alone. The problems are the shared responsibility of humankind and cry out for solutions that, like the problems themselves, also cross frontiers. The UN exists to find these solutions through the common endeavor of all states. It is the indispensable global organization for a globalizing world.

Large portions of the world's population require the UN's assistance to surmount problems they cannot overcome on their own. As these words are written, civil war rages in Congo and Liberia and sputters in Côte d'Ivoire, while long-running conflicts may be close to permanent solution in Cyprus and Sierra Leone. The arduous task of nation building proceeds fitfully in Afghanistan, the Balkans, East Timor, and Iraq. Twenty million refugees and displaced persons, from Palestine to Liberia and beyond, depend on the UN for shelter and succor. Decades of development in Africa are being wiped out by the scourge of HIVAIDS (and its deadly interaction with famine and drought), and the Millennium Development Goals—agreed on with much fanfare in September 2000, at the UN's Millennium Summit, the largest gathering of heads of government in human history—remain unfulfilled. Too many countries still lack the wherewithal to eliminate poverty, educate girls, safeguard health, and provide their people with clean drinking water. If the UN did not exist to help tackle these problems, they would undoubtedly end up on the doorstep of the world's only superpower. . . .

Whether one is from Tashkent or Tallahassee, it is simply not realistic to think only of one's own country. Global forces press in from every conceivable direction; people, goods, and ideas cross borders and cover vast distances with ever greater frequency, speed, and ease. The Internet is emblematic of an era in which what happens in Southeast Asia or southern Africa-from democratic advances to deforestation to the fight against AIDS-can affect Americans. As has been observed about water pollution, we all live downstream now. . . .

At the same time, the concept of the nation-state as self-sufficient has also weakened; although the state remains the primary political unit, most citizens now instinctively understand that it cannot do everything on its own. To function in the world, people increasingly have to deal with institutions and individuals beyond their country's borders. American jobs depend not only on local firms and factories, but also on faraway markets, grants of licenses and access from foreign governments,

Whether one is from Tashkent or Tallahassee, it is simply not realistic to think only of one's own country. . . . The Internet is emblematic of an era in which what happens in Southeast Asia or southern Africa-from democratic advances to deforestation to the fight against AIDS-can affect Americans. As has been observed about water pollution, we all live downstream now. . . .

—Shashi Tharoor

As the World Health Organization's successful battle against the dreaded SARS epidemic has demonstrated, "problems without passports" are those that only international action can solve....

—Shashi Tharoor

international trade rules that ensure the free movement of goods and persons, and international financial institutions that ensure stability. There are thus few unilateralists in the American business community. Americans' safety, meanwhile, depends not only on local police forces, but also on guarding against the global spread of pollution, disease, terror, illegal drugs, and WMD [weapons of mass destruction]. As the World Health Organization's successful battle against the dreaded SARS epidemic has demonstrated, "problems without passports" are those that only international action can solve. . . .

Technological Interdependence
Thomas P. Hughes

Technology is not value free. It expresses the values of its creators and users. San Francisco's Golden Gate Bridge is a statement of civic pride. The new Central Artery and Tunnel Bridge across the Charles River from Boston to Cambridge is also a proud civic symbol.

Technology often expresses and cultivates interdependence as a value. A good example of technological interdependence is the Pennsylvania-New Jersey Interconnection (PNJ), a complex, federated, networked, interdependent, electric power system.

—Thomas P. Hughes

Technology often expresses and cultivates interdependence as a value. A good example of technological interdependence is the Pennsylvania-New Jersey Interconnection (PNJ), a complex, federated, networked, interdependent, electric power system. Established in 1925, the PNJ initially connected the Philadelphia Electric Company, the Public Service Electric & Gas Company of New Jersey, and the Pennsylvania Power and Light Company.

Physically the interconnection involved a 200-mile long, 220,000-volt, circular trunk transmission line to which the three utilities connected. Each utility fed energy into the trunk line or removed energy from it according to the load each carried at a particular time. Because the three utilities had peak loads at different times, they could exchange power advantageously. If one of the utilities was heavily loaded in the late evening hours, for example, and another had a light power load then, the lightly loaded would feed power into the interconnection and the heavily loaded would take power from it.

Inventing the management-by-committee structure of the PNJ proved more complicated than designing the physical layout. Each utility sent several representatives to periodic committee meetings where members negotiated the price each would charge to the PNJ when supplying energy to the system and the price each would pay when taking energy from it. The federated utilities retained their autonomy despite their interdependence.

By analogy, we can imagine an interconnected and interdependent system of nation states. Each nation would pool its networked resources, such as electric power, telecommunications, and Internet. Because of time and societal differences among the nations, they could feed resources into the network or remove them according to need. As in the case of the PNJ, each nation would have representatives on an administrative committee. Ideally, they would decide by consensus the price each would pay to take resources from the pools and the remuneration each would receive for supplying them to the pools.

The nation-state infrastructure systems might well nurture a generalized commitment to interdependence because of national dependence on the transnational technological infrastructure. Nations with their electric power, telecommunications, and Internet infrastructures integrated would find it difficult to function independently in both peacetime and in wartime.

Since World War II, European nations have created technologically interdependent systems that are fostering interdependence in other realms. A single electric-supply system connects Finland, Norway, Sweden, and Eastern Denmark. This Nordic system links to the entire European system. In the 1970s the Soviet Union began exporting natural gas to Western Europe, which Russia continues to do. Its exports to Europe in 2001 amounted to 25 percent of the European Union's imports. Optimists argue that this will encourage peaceful relations. In the realm of transportation, the Channel Tunnel opened in 1994 connects Britain and France for the first time since the Ice Age, and the Oresund Bridge completed about the same time links Denmark and Sweden. Underwater telecommunication cables throughout the world have fostered interdependence for more than a century.

Technological interdependence expresses the will of nations and organizations that highly value interdependence for a variety of reasons; including the quest for economic advantage and the wish to promote peaceful relations.

Published with permission of the author.

Technological interdependence expresses the will of nations and organizations that highly value interdependence for a variety of reasons; including the quest for economic advantage and the wish to promote peaceful relations.

—*Thomas P. Hughes*

Religion and Interdependence
Patrice C. Brodeur

The deep connection between religion and interdependence can be described in at least five ways: linguistically, historically, philosophically, ethically, and spiritually.

Linguistically, the root meaning of 'religion' is 'to connect', 'to join together' (Latin: *religare*). This word evolved in both form and meaning over more than two thousand years. By continuing to use the word 'religion', we live in linguistic interdependence with its various meanings over time, many of which continue to exist today. For some people, religion simply means a set of rituals and beliefs in a higher power that guides people's lives; for others, it means institutions that provide collective sacred meaning and purpose. The word 'religions' in the plural appeared only in the 18th century in reference to different worldviews that shared the idea of a transcendent reality, whether called God, the Divine, or the state of nirvana. We now use both the genus 'religion' in the singular and the species 'religions' in the plural. The latter includes, for example, Baha'ism, Buddhism, Confucianism, Christianity, Hinduism, Islam, Judaism, Sikhism, Taoism, and Zoroastrianism.

Historically, religions have existed interdependently, though not all at once. Religious people have identified with one or more religions whose boundaries are often porous. When a person or group of persons started to differ significantly from the majority interpretation within one religion, it often resulted in the founding of a new division within it or sometimes what came to be understood later as a new religion altogether. Even as separate religions, religious people and communities have continued to influence each other mutually to different degrees: the greater the geographical proximity, the greater their interdependence has been. This old historical principle is now changing, however, as more access to cyberspace is turning our whole planet into a global village. Geographical proximity is no longer the only way to measure interdependence.

Philosophically, religious communities have developed their respective worldviews or theologies to interpret intellectually their members' individual and collective experiences of reality. These interpretations, often understood as based on or deriving from the transcendent reality they believe in, use the language and concepts current at the time and place where they have emerged, reflecting the contextual interdependence of both people and ideas.

Ethically, religious people have nurtured deep moral commitments to mostly shared values and principles such as the search for truth in one's life and in the world, the cultivation of compassion for others, and the promotion of integrity in personal human behavior and of justice in collective interactions. These overlapping moral commitments are now being examined to increase our understanding of the ethical interdependence within a wide range of religious people and communities and between them and people who define themselves in terms other than religious ones. This new trend has given rise to important interreligious and inter-ideological cooperation for peace and justice around the world; a sign of our increasing self-reflective human interdependence.

Spiritually, religious communities have nurtured spaces where, through their integrated worldviews and rituals, the mystical experience of ultimate reality becomes possible; the individual self dissolves, thereby moving beyond interdependence of parts (self versus others) to a unity of pure and undivided consciousness.

Religion, as both concept and experience, mirrors the reality of interdependence in all spheres of life.

Published with permission of the author.

Liberal Education and Global Community
Martha Nussbaum

. . . The idea of liberal education is more important than ever in our interdependent world. An education based on the idea of an inclusive global citizenship and on the possibilities of the compassionate imagination has the potential to transcend divisions created by distance, cultural difference, and mistrust. Developing this ideal further and thinking about how to modify it in the light of our times is one of the most exciting and urgent tasks we can undertake as educators and citizens.

We live in a time of fear. Since 9/11, Americans have had to face the vulnerability of our towers, our pride, even our chosen institutions and way of life. Fear narrows the moral imagination, making it difficult to view with sympathy the situation of people who live at a distance or who look different from ourselves. Fear leads to polarization. In place of a variegated world of human beings pursuing a wide range of projects out of a wide range of needs, a world of complex interdependencies and of shared problems, fear constructs a simpler world, a world that consists of the vulnerable yet all-important Us and the dark, besieging Them.

Polarization does real harm to our relationships with other nations and with groups inside our own society. The metaphor of a "conflict of civilizations" springs easily to people's minds and lips, obscuring the human needs of people in developing countries, obscuring the complexity and heterogeneity of Islam worldwide, obscuring the variety of needs, beliefs, and interests in the developing world as a whole.

To counter these pernicious tendencies, we need accurate global knowledge and habits of self-criticism. We need theories of global justice and policies that implement these theories. But we need something more fundamental: the compassionate

...The idea of liberal education is more important than ever in our interdependent world. An education based on the idea of an inclusive global citizenship and on the possibilities of the compassionate imagination has the potential to transcend divisions created by distance, cultural difference, and mistrust.

—*Martha Nussbaum*

imagination, which can make other people's lives more than distant abstractions. How can we educate American citizens who do take seriously the reality of lives outside America, and who think of political events accordingly? And what role does our tradition of liberal education at the college and university level play in this process of forming imaginative and compassionate world citizens? Why is this idea more important now than ever?

All nations face problems of religious and ethnic antagonism internally, and all face our world's growing cultural and religious tensions in international relations. In the case of the nations of Europe, sudden changes in the numbers of immigrants, together with dropping birthrates, are making heterogeneity a fact of life in a way that perhaps it was not before. Suddenly, these nations are recognizing that their curricula for higher education do nothing to form citizens for a pluralistic society and an interlocking world. Programs in ethnic studies and women's studies have sprung up, but unless students want to take a whole degree in those subjects, something that is not likely to lead to good employment options, they are likely to have little contact with these programs. Hence, the American idea [of liberal education] begins to look increasingly attractive, and, indeed, urgent.

Given . . . the climate of fear and polarization in the United States, this idea has become more important than ever for Americans, as we struggle to position ourselves in a world that is interdependent, in which only international cooperation will solve problems of hunger, disease, and environmental degradation and produce the possibility of a stable peace among nations. Because America is so dominant, it is easy for Americans to go through life in a bubble of American-ness, speaking English and rarely venturing out of the secure setting of American culture, even when we travel. Only liberal education has the potential to undo these baneful and complacent habits of mind, producing global citizens who can think well about the problems of today's world.

Liberal education is attractive to both Americans and non-Americans, because it places the accent on the creation of a critical public culture, through an emphasis on analytical thinking, argumentation, and active participation in debate.

[The] concept of a link between liberal education and a deeper and more inclusive kind of citizenship has a special urgency in these times, for young citizens in all nations. It certainly has a special urgency for Americans, as we struggle with the burdens of being American in an era of American domination, asking ourselves what we owe to the rest of the world, how we can rightly take our place in international debates of many sorts. Americans especially often link up to the rest of the world through a very thin set of connections: In particular, as consumers and people involved in business, we connect to the rest of the world above all through a global market that sees human lives as instruments for gain. If institutions of higher education do not build a richer network of human connections it is likely that our dealings with one another will be mediated by the impoverished norms of market exchange and profit making. And these impoverished norms do not help, to put it mildly, if what we want is a world of peace, where people will be able to live fruitful, cooperative lives.

Cultivating our humanity in a complex interlocking world involves understanding the ways in which common needs and aims are differently realized in different circumstances. This requires a great deal of knowledge that American college students rarely got in previous eras. I believe that it is urgent that all undergraduates should be led into the rudiments of world history and a basic understanding of the major world religions. They should then learn to inquire in more depth into at least one unfamiliar culture. We must become more curious and more humble about our role in the world, and we will do this only if undergraduate education is reformed in this direction.

One further point that I would like to underline is that the study of a foreign language is an extremely important part of developing this sort of global understanding. Even if the language is that of a relatively familiar culture, the sheer activity of seeing the world from the viewpoint of another culture's ways of carving it up and expressing what is important in it, the sheer understanding of why translation is always imperfect and a reinterpretation, is humbling, and the best reminder there can be that not all intelligent people have the same view of life.

Imaginative Understanding

Citizens cannot think well on the basis of factual knowledge alone. [We need to cultivate] . . . the narrative imagination . . . the ability to think what it might be like to be in the shoes of a person different from oneself, to be an intelligent reader of that person's story, and to understand the emotions and wishes and desires that someone so placed might have. These capacities for imaginative and emotional understanding are developed by literature and the other arts. The great John Dewey long ago argued that the arts were modes of intelligent perception and experience that should play a crucial role in education, forming the civic imagination. Even before him, Rousseau argued that young Emile would only become a good citizen, with compassion for the poor and the downtrodden, if he did have an education nourished by the narrative imagination of human predicaments.

Courses in literature and the arts can impart this ability in many ways, through engagement with many different works of literature, music, fine arts, and dance. . . .We need to cultivate our students' "inner eyes," to use a phrase of Ralph Ellison's. This means carefully crafted courses in the arts and humanities, which bring students into contact with issues of gender, race, ethnicity, and cross-cultural experience and understanding.

> Citizens cannot think well on the basis of factual knowledge alone. [We need to cultivate] . . . the narrative imagination . . . the ability to think what it might be like to be in the shoes of a person different from oneself . . .
>
> —*Martha Nussbaum*

> . . . only an education that reveals our common human strivings and our common human vulnerabilities, challenging us to see the distance truly, can lead us into a world of peace and global cooperation.
>
> —*Martha Nussbaum*

Liberal education is in one way frightening. For it requires opening the personality to change and questioning, to the possibility of moving out of the security of one's own comforting habits. But only an education that reveals our common human strivings and our common human vulnerabilities, challenging us to see the distance truly, can lead us into a world of peace and global cooperation.

from *Changing Minds*
Howard Gardner

On rare occasions, individuals with neither vast armies nor vast congregations have succeeded in exerting influence well beyond national boundaries. . . . They have done so because of the persuasiveness of their stories and the steadfastness with which they have reinforced those stories through their manner of living. In the twentieth century, three men stand out as exemplars in this category: Mohandas (Mahatma) Gandhi, Nelson Mandela, and Jean Monnet.

Perhaps the most well-known is Gandhi. Growing up in undistinguished surroundings in late-nineteenth-century colonial India, Gandhi spent time in England as a young man and then lived for twenty years in South Africa. There he was horrified by the mistreatment by European colonizers of Indians and other "colored persons"; he read widely in philosophy and religion; and he became involved in various protests. Returning to his native India at the start of the World War I Gandhi perfected methods of satyagraha—peaceful (nonviolent) protest (or resistance). . . . Gandhi led a series of strikes and protest marches, destined to throw into sharp relief the differences between the brutal English masters—who sought to hold power at any cost—and the nonbelligerent Indians. These protests where choreographed to underscore the nobility of the native cause and the reasonableness with which Indians were striving to express their goals. Gandhi's overt message was: "We do not seek to make war or shed blood. We only want to be treated as fellow human beings. Once we have achieved the status of equals, we have no further claims."

In one sense, Gandhi's message could not have been simpler: It can be traced back to Christ and to other religious leaders. Yet, it also clashed with an entrenched counterstory: that one can only attain an equal status vis-á-vis one's colonizers if—like the United States in the late eighteenth century or South America in the early nineteenth century—one is willing to go to war. Moreover, Gandhi did not only have a simple linguistic message; he also developed an integrated program of prayer, fasting, and facing one's opponents without weapons, even willing to do so until death. His embodiment of the message could not have been more dramatic; it went well beyond verbal expression, to include a wide range of evocative formats, such as his squatting on the ground and operating a simple machine for spinning cloth.

Gandhi's story reverberated around the world. While annoying some (Churchill memorably disparaged him as that "half-naked fakir"), it inspired many leaders and ordinary citizens—ranging from Martin Luther King Jr. in the American South in the early 1960s, to the students who rallied for greater democracy in Tiananmen Square in Beijing in 1989.

Like Gandhi, Nelson Mandela embodied a message that resonated on a level far beyond the borders of his own South Africa. Indeed, of all the leaders in recent years, Mandela is widely considered one of the most impressive and influential. A lawyer by training, Mandela became actively involved in resistance as part of the African National Congress. At first he embraced nonviolent resistance, but after a series of frustrating and degrading encounters, he joined a paramilitary group. Narrowly escaping death by combat or judicial sentence, Mandela was imprisoned for twenty-seven years. Although such an experience would likely have demoralized, radicalized, or marginalize most other persons—especially since it occurred at middle age, often considered the apogee of an individual's personal power—imprisonment seemed only to fortify Mandela. On his release, he rejected any effort to engage in armed conflict; instead he worked with his political opponent F.W. de Klerk to set up democratic institutions, and in 1994 he went on to win the presidency of a post-apartheid South Africa.

Rather than seeking revenge against this opponents and jailers, Mandela called for reconciliation. He was convinced—and was able to convince others—that South Africa could not function as a society unless it could put its wrenching history behind it. Under the leadership of Nobel Peace Prize winner Archbishop Desmond Tutu, Mandela convened a Truth and Reconciliation Commission. The Gandhian idea behind this commission was that it would seek to establish what actually happened during the years of apartheid but would not attempt to sit in ultimate judgment. The truth having been established as well as it could be, citizens of varying persuasions could come to terms with the past and commit their future energies to the buildup of a new and more fully representative society. A master of nonverbal as well as verbal forms, Mandela asked his one-time jailer to sit in the first row during his presidential inaugural ceremony.

Mandela succeeded in changing the minds not only of millions of his otherwise diverse fellow citizens but equally of millions of observers around the world—few of whom would have predicted that South Africa could become a new nation without decades of bloodshed. Ideas like the Truth and Reconciliation Commission have traveled across national boundaries. The tipping points for Mandela's success entail

On rare occasions, individuals with neither vast armies nor vast congregations have succeeded in exerting influence well beyond national boundaries.... They have done so because of the persuasiveness of their stories and the steadfastness with which they have reinforced those stories through their manner of living.

—*Howard Gardner*

both his exemplary behavior after his release from jail and the willingness of the entrenched South African leadership to negotiate with him—both examples reflecting Mandela's personal resonance, among other things.

A third figure of global importance worked largely behind the scenes; the French economist and diplomat Jean Monnet, born in 1888. When his comfortable life was shattered by the events of World War I, Monnet—a careful and reflective student of history—pondered why it was necessary for European countries to continue to go to war, as they had intermittently since the time of Charlemagne more than a thousand years before. He began to work toward the creation of institutions that could bring about a united Europe. After the trauma of World War I, the collapse of the League of Nations, the rise of fascism, and the unprecedented warfare of World War II, a lesser person would have concluded that attempts to build a European community were futile. Monnet, however, was a firm believer in his own oft-repeated slogan: "I regard every defeat (or every challenge) as an opportunity." Amid the physical and psychological ruins of war-torn Europe, Monnet envisioned—and proceeded to sow—the seeds of a larger European polity.

Unlike a president, a pope, or the leader of an international organization such as the United Nations, neither Gandhi, nor Mandela, nor Monnet had a dedicated, guaranteed audience. They had to create their constituencies from scratch, with neither financial inducements nor coercive political weapons. They had to identify and speak to an opposition that held power: leaders of South Africa and colonial India, in Gandhi's case; the defenders of apartheid in Mandela's case; and the entrenched national interests of Europe in Monnet's case. At the same time they had to address and convince a lay constituency. Neither Gandhi nor Mandela could have led the fight for independence without an "army" of ordinary followers, who, in the extreme, were prepared to die nonviolently for their cause. And while Monnet worked significantly behind the scenes in the manner of what I term an "indirect" leader, his vision of Europe ultimately has had to triumph at the ballot box.

. . . These men had available only the weapons of persuasion and embodiment. They had to tell their stories over and over again, tell them well, and embody their stories in appropriate life actions and evocative symbolic elements. They had to recognize, acknowledge, and ultimately undermine the regnant counterstories. And it is here that they showed their genius.

from The Lesson of Hannah Arendt

Samantha Power

. . . In *Origins*[1] Arendt offered contradictory impressions of the nation-state. In her discussions of anti-Semitism and imperialism, she pronounced the nation-state's imminent demise. Yet in her discussion of twentieth-century human rights abusers, she suggested that it was the durability of the nation-state that boded ill for the persecuted. It is difficult to discern what Arendt herself wished for states. It was clear that governments could not be counted on to prevent suffering inside their borders, or to redress suffering outside. The excluded, the poor, the powerless, the stateless, would regularly be left orphaned by a community of well-wishing liberal internationalists. Yet the very selfishness of states also meant that human beings were most likely to see their rights enforced if they looked not to some abstract international community, but to their own governments. If this was true, she seemed to suggest, then however poisonous the track record of states, only they could offer inclusive, enforceable constitutional protections and remedies for their citizens.

Arendt's suspicions about the false promise of liberal internationalism were well-founded, but what she underestimated was the intrinsic appeal of human rights principles around the world—a resonance that has resulted more in the bottom-up promotion of human rights than in the top-down protection envisaged in 1948. In 1975, when Arendt died, Amnesty International, which had been founded in 1961, had an annual budget of $860,000. Arendt could not have envisaged a day when a nonstate entity like Human Rights Watch would spend more than $22 million per year, and would conduct its own rigorous field investigations to shame criminal officials, their abettors, and the world's bystanders. And far more important than international human rights groups are the hundreds of thousands of indigenous human rights groups—led by labor organizers, women's suffrage advocates, AIDS activists, fledgling independent newspaper journalists, and others—throughout the developing world. It is with these groups that hope lies. It is these committed and engaged people who have the most at stake in their countries' futures, and who see themselves not as "human beings in general," but as political actors who may eventually ensure that election results are respected, the military and police are restrained, and individual rights are enforced. . . .

In some countries state control is so fierce that independent voices are silenced and marginalized, power and wealth are concentrated among elites, and injustice flourishes. In others, war or occupation has brought such ruin and humiliation that civil society cannot emerge and no amount of organizing can restore living standards or human dignity. It is from some of these countries that contemporary terrorist

> It is . . . committed and engaged people who have the most at stake in their countries' futures, and who see themselves not as "human beings in general," but as political actors who may eventually ensure that election results are respected, the military and police are restrained, and individual rights are enforced. . . .
>
> —*Samantha Power*

---

1 Arendt, Hannah. *The Origins of Totalitarianism.*

threats come, and it is here that *Origins* offers further wisdom for today's dark times—wisdom that we ignore at our peril.

Militant Islam is not well understood by those who feel most threatened by it. Some of its legions of followers have been drawn by the exclusionary and radical conservatism of its vision; others have been attracted by a sense of belonging, a desire for power, or a hunger for revenge. Those who have flocked to terrorist organizations have faith—in religion, or in an ideology that can double as a religion. If one could pierce the veil of mystery that shrouds al-Qaeda, Hamas, or Islamic Jihad, one might well find some of the qualities Arendt associated with totalitarian movements:

> Supreme disregard for immediate consequences rather than ruthlessness; rootlessness and neglect of national interests rather than nationalism; contempt for utilitarian motives rather than unconsidered pursuit of self-interest; "idealism," i.e., their unwavering faith in an ideological fictitious world, rather than lust for power.

Arendt wrote of German and Soviet selfless devotion to the idealized collective, but what greater testament to such selflessness can there be but martyrdom of the kind that thousands of young Muslim men and women are queuing up to undertake today?

In the United States since September 11, 2001, Americans have begun asking, "Why do they hate us?" The response tends to fall between two extremes. Bush administration officials say, in effect, they hate us for who we are. As President Bush has put it, "They hate progress, and freedom, and choice, and culture, and music, and laughter, and women, and Christians, and Jews, and all Muslims who reject their distorted doctrines."[2] Adherents of this view ignore the devastating impact of specific US policies on those who have learned to hate. At the opposite extreme stand those who insist that young men and women are flocking to martyr themselves exclusively because of what the United States has done. They cite uncritical US support for Israel, its backing of corrupt and repressive Middle Eastern states, and its exploitation of the world's natural resources. But adherents of this position often ignore the role played by a variety of other social, political, and economic factors in contributing to local misery.

Arendt would likely avoid both rigid views and summon us to do three things simultaneously: meet the threat abroad, preserve essential freedoms at home, and be unafraid to explore the motives and aims of the enemy. In meeting the threat, she would argue that lethal collective movements cannot be met with words alone, but must also be met with force. As one disgusted by the convenient patience and wishful thinking of European statesmen before and during the Holocaust, Arendt would

---

2 President George W. Bush, address to the corps of cadets at the Citadel, December 11, 2001.

undoubtedly urge us to rid ourselves of our "common-sense disinclination to believe the monstrous" and make all necessary sacrifices to guard against chemical attacks, dirty bombs, and other atrocities that our imaginations can hardly dare to broach. But while Arendt valued what today is termed "hard power," she also knew first-hand the danger of state overreaching in the name of self-defense, and the prospect that a merciless "counter-ideology" could emerge. Today, in the name of fighting a war of infinite duration, it has again proven far too tempting for our liberal democracy to give security absolute priority over liberty, slighting or scrapping the values so central to American constitutionalism, and surrendering before a new ideology of counterterrorism.

Origins shows that Arendt would not be satisfied with a policy that aimed to violently crush today's threat without seeking to understand it. In the preface to *Origins*, she set out "to discover the hidden mechanics by which all traditional elements of our political and spiritual world were dissolved," leading to a situation "unrecognizable for human comprehension." We have landed in a similarly unimaginable place today. Yet thus far, in their desire to avoid legitimating a murderous cause by considering its origins, our leaders have refused to try to understand the hidden mechanics of how we got to where we are. Arendt used the phrase "radical evil" to describe totalitarianism, and this is an idea that has been brought back into circulation. Yet while Arendt did not allow such branding to deter her from exploring the sources of that evil, the less subtle minds who invoke the concept today do so to mute criticisms of their responses. (Who, after all, can be against combatting evil?)

But sheltering behind black-and-white characterizations is not only questionable for moral or epistemological reasons. It poses a practical problem because it blinds us from understanding and thus undermines our long-term ability to prevent and surmount what we don't know and most fear. "Evil," whether radical or banal, is met most often with unimaginativeness. Terrorism is a threat that demands a complex and elaborate effort to distinguish the sympathizers from the militants and to keep its converts to a minimum. Terrorism also requires understanding how our past policies helped give rise to such venomous grievances. *Origins* is chilling to read today because it reveals that even the most radical evils, Nazism and Stalinism, were driven by an internal logic and a self-perceived morality. It simply has to be true, given the human costs and nuclear stakes of the contemporary showdown, that we can never know too much about terrorist movements, and that we can never try too hard to alleviate the indignities and inequalities that may help fuel the threat.

Hannah Arendt had what W.B. Yeats called the uncommon ability "to hold in a single thought reality and justice." In Arendt's preface to *Origins*, she noted:

> This book has been written against a background both of reckless optimism and reckless despair. It holds that Progress and Doom are two sides of the same medal; that both are articles of superstition, not of faith.

Today, in the name of fighting a war of infinite duration, it has again proven far too tempting for our liberal democracy to give security absolute priority over liberty, slighting or scrapping the values so central to American constitutionalism, and surrendering before a new ideology of counterterrorism.

—*Samantha Power*

In order to move beyond superstition, which is what we cling to today, it is politics that has to be brought to bear. We are afraid, and fear is dangerous. It can justify excesses and can lead to escapism. The gravest temptation is an overwhelmed, apolitical retreat into private life. But it is not enough to lament the burden of our time; we citizens must shape the response. It is only in the public sphere, through voting, voicing, and mobilizing, that our fates become our own. While fear is dangerous, fear can also concentrate the mind and lead citizens to take political action. The coming years—where we find ourselves again suspended "between a no-longer and a not-yet."[3]—are years of danger and promise, and we can only hope, as Arendt did, that the tug toward apathy will be overcome by the lure of human improvement and self-preservation.

Reprinted with the permission of the Wylie Agency Inc. From *The New York Review of Books*. Volume 51, Number 7. April 29, 2004. p. 34–37. Copyright © 2003 by Samantha Power.

Young Voices

My Responsibility
Tariq Adwan

As the world becomes smaller, the need for recognizing, respecting and understanding differences among peoples and cultures is of the greatest importance. The world has become so transparent that information, events and activities are widely accessible. At the same time human and natural resources are distributed unevenly all over the world; no nation-state has them all. These realities make interdependence among nations, peoples, cultures, and individuals a necessity. We complement each other by what we have and who we are: black or white or red, rich or poor, Christians, Jews, Muslims or other believers, social or natural scientists, males or females.

Thinking about interdependence makes us realize how much we need each other. It helps to reduce stereotypes, enmity and hatred, and increases the chances of peace and coexistence. Interdependence is when you and I feel that our lives and our dignity are of equally high value. For me interdependence represents the end of mental barriers among nations and individuals in the world; it's when people think beyond geographical borders—as citizens of the earth, not only of a particular country.

---

2 Hannah Arendt, *Men in Dark Times* (Harcourt, Brace and World, 1968), p. 90.

I have been living in the United States for almost three years, going to college. When I first came, I realized how little I knew about American culture and history, and its social and political life. It still amazes me how little Americans know about my culture. It seems that my American friends and I were totally shielded from each other before we met, even though we are from the same planet.

Being a Palestinian and living under Israeli occupation all my life, I have always been concerned about how to establish myself as a Palestinian citizen and how to protect and maintain my Palestinian identity. I was so busy doing that that I forgot about myself as a citizen of the world.

It's hard for Palestinians to think they are part of this world when they are being isolated by walls. Our freedom of movement is very restricted. How can we think that we are a part of the world when the concrete walls around us are so high that we can't even see the house on the other side of the wall?

In an interdependent world, you can hear about people's suffering in other parts of the world. I think that's the most important step toward establishing global peace. Oppressed peoples want to be heard; they need to know they are not living in a vacuum; that there are people in other parts of the world who are trying to help them. That certainly gives them a positive view of the world. Our civic responsibility is not only for people of the same nationality, but for people of the same race—the human race. It's not just a courtesy to think of the benefit of others, its our duty. We must always remember that conflicts in the Far East affect the lives of people in the Far West. We have been more concerned about establishing equality among people within the same geographical boundaries; now its time to establish equality among people worldwide.

As a science major in a pre-med course, my future responsibility is to help improve the quality of life and health for humans worldwide; therefore I feel its my duty to have a broad understanding of health-related issues not only in my country but also in the rest of the world. Scientists from all parts of the world have been very efficient in collaborating to make this world healthier and safer, despite political, religious and cultural differences. I see it as my duty to carry this scientific collaboration further in the coming years, to make sure every person in the world gets equal health care—not because I am nice person but because it's their right—and its my responsibility.

Published with permission of the author.

> Interdependence is when you and I feel that our lives and our dignity are of equally high value.
>
> —*Tariq Adwan*

> Our civic responsibility is not only for people of the same nationality, but for people of the same race—the human race.
>
> —*Tariq Adwan*

Interdependence Speaks
Lilly Deng

I was born in 1987 in a rural Chinese factory town. My parents spent their teen years under the political oppression of the Cultural Revolution, and in adulthood, they watched the violence at Tiananmen Square. As a result, they were suspicious of government as an agent of protection.

Growing up in America, I had a very different experience. I was young and civic-minded, believing that we could change the world simply by petitioning legislators. Such naïveté, however, exists only in the absence of experience, and when I was twelve, an extended stay in China disabused me of my rampant idealism. I learned that life is not an either/or situation. It's much more complicated.

In America, the impetus for responsible decision-making is clear: laws made of, for, and by the people, a voting citizenry, media exposure, and the creative tension between the branches of government. I actually knew my senators and representatives, whereas among my Chinese peers, there was little knowledge of political processes or where to find more information. Most unusual to me was visiting Beijing, where all streets were closed for five hours on a Saturday night, when military tanks passed through and people stood on the edge of the streets, unable to cross. More alarming than the actual halting of foot traffic was that people felt no impulse to question it. Such events, interrupting their lives, were commonplace.

Still, despite the communistic framework, there were many local and familial values in China that I appreciated. A strong sense of heritage encouraged most people to live within the region of their birth, where relatives were only a bus stop away. Even distant family members gathered weekly, and children were raised together with their cousins. On any day of the week, one could take a walk and see scores of people on the streets practicing Tai-Chi, playing mah-jongg, or reading.

> I have learned from both my American and Chinese experiences that social and political advancement can occur only when the dominant government structure allows for cultural expression. Globalization must not replace existing norms, values and culture; it must protect and reaffirm them.
>
> —*Lilly Deng*

I have learned from both my American and Chinese experiences that social and political advancement can occur only when the dominant government structure allows for cultural expression. Globalization must not replace existing norms, values and culture; it must protect and reaffirm them. And newly gained rights cannot be exercised if they are inconsistent with or inaccessible to the general standard of living. Paper freedoms are likely to be set aside for more tangible material gains unless people develop the civic will and skills to enjoy them and recognize the responsibility that comes with them.

The United States has the great advantage of a multi-ethnic mix that spans every corner of the globe, and resources that are incomparable to other countries. In our unique position, it is possible for interdependence to expand beyond the economic and environmental ties that bind us to others to include the cultural ties as well. We must recognize that others have qualities similar to our own, respect beneficial foreign ideologies, and commit ourselves to using our experiences to promote the understanding and actions that build a genuine global community.

Published with permission of the author.

Interdependence Must be Natural
Zamira Djabarova

When I started to write this essay I asked my father what interdependence means to him? He said, "The Soviet Union was an excellent example of interdependence. Look how interconnected and interdependent the fifteen member countries were. Let's take our aluminum processing plant in Tajikstan as an example. It brought raw material from Russia and send it back to Russia after processing. And the city of Ivanovo, one of the biggest centers of Russia's textile industry, imported all its cotton from the Central Asian countries. We learned the Tajik aluminum processing plant can't do anything without Russian aluminum, and the Ivanovo factories have nothing to work on without Central Asian cotton.

And then I said: "But as a result of such interdependence, the costs of goods were much higher."

His answer was: "Within the Soviet system, the ends justified the means. In order to keep the Union intact, the states were forced to depend on each other.

I wasn't happy with his answer. It made me probe deeper into interdependence. Is the Soviet Union an example of interdependence? Well, yes, it is, but it's an unnatural, forced interdependence. Now that the Soviet Union has collapsed, and states are not forced to be interdependent anymore, what do we have? Armies of unemployed people. Tajikistan is a source of raw materials, which doesn't create a lot of job opportunities; but it doesn't have enough money to build factories and plants. So the collapsed Soviet Union is really a good example of how a *forced* interdependence doesn't work. But there is another way for interdependence. Throughout the 20th century and even now, nations have fought for independence—which means they don't want to be dependent. So, one-way dependency doesn't really work. But today, we see trans-state organizations and different kinds of cooperatives among the former Soviet states, which demonstrates that they are not against interdependence. They were against an interdependence forced upon them from above.

Interdependence that is realized and voluntarily accepted as an alternative to independence, is something which seems to work. We recognize that complete independence is impossible, it is simply not a reality. And so we've come to acknowledge our reality—it is interdependence. Building on that reality. I think we can make our world a better place. We can create a truly dynamic interdependence which can make these states stronger politically and economically.

Published with permission of the author.

> Interdependence that is realized and voluntarily accepted as an alternative to independence, is something which seems to work. We recognize that complete independence is impossible, it is simply not a reality.
>
> —*Zamira Djabarova*

The Challenge of a Generation
Josh Goldstein

Over 200 people packed the Grand Ballroom of the University of Maryland-College Park's Student Center on a rainy Friday afternoon, September 12th, 2003, to hear a panel discussion on "Global Citizenship: The Challenge of a Generation," marking the first Interdependence Day.

Eyes were fixed on the table in the front of the room, where five students sat and spoke about their work connecting their local community with the most important global issues. Throughout the day, close to 1000 people would attend three Interdependence Day events, including a morning community service event with the Mayor of College Park and an evening concert featuring local and national hip hop artists. As the panel came to a close and students in the audience excitedly approached me to talk about the projects they had been working on, I began to realize the true importance of the Interdependence project.

Interdependence is everywhere. On nearly every campus there are hands-on projects that address everything from fair-trade coffee to food and healthcare in Africa. What is lacking is an understanding that these projects all work under the same assumption, that in the ever-smalling globalized world, the actions of one community can have a lasting effect on the entire world.

The goal of Interdependence Day is two-fold. First, it is to create a space for an open dialogue on campus about our ideas of global citizenship, and how our generation will think about an expanded idea of community. The dialogue can take many forms, including academic panels with professors, politicians, students, and activists taking part, and/or student roundtable discussions and town meetings.

Second, Interdependence Day provides a showcase of each community's existing tools for global citizenship. The events of the day bring a renewed energy, generating new ideas for expansion to those who are already deeply involved in important work. Further, it gives students who have never been involved an inspiration and a tangible way of getting started. No event I have seen in my college career so actively encouraged both thought and action as Interdependence Day.

While the first Interdependence Day was celebrated only on American campuses, interest in the second annual event has spread to students on every continent in the world. Only now, thanks to the Internet, is it possible for students to work together on such a large scale. And it is now that there is so much need to use all the resources at our command to create a global civic community; and it is now that our generation can and must step up to the plate.

Published with permission of the author.

Interdependence Day provides a showcase of each community's existing tools for global citizenship. The events of the day bring a renewed energy, generating new ideas for expansion to those who are already deeply involved in important work.

—*Josh Goldstein*

Bringing the World Back Together
Seth Green

It is fitting that September 12 has been designated Interdependence Day. If September 11, 2001 illustrated the new dangers of our interconnectedness, September 12, 2001 demonstrated the wonders of our increasingly globalized world. In the aftermath of that horrific September morning, people around the world expressed their heartfelt sympathy. As a young American studying abroad soon after the terrorist attacks, I was pleasantly surprised when strangers in the streets of London heard my accent and stopped me to share their grief. It seemed as if everyone I met, from Parisians to Pakistanis, were New Yorkers at heart.

But over the years that followed the terrorist attacks of September 11, 2001 that immense goodwill vanished. Instead of being seen as a defensive ally protecting the world against terror, the U.S. came to be viewed as the aggressor. Deeply concerned by America's diminishing image abroad and its consequences, I joined with other Americans abroad to establish a nonpartisan organization called Americans for Informed Democracy (AID). AID sought to organize forums where Americans could engage in collaborative discussions on issues ranging from Iraq to Islam with our international peers.

On September 12, 2003, AID worked with *Dialogues: Islamic World–U.S.–the West* and the Institute for International Mediation and Conflict Resolution to coordinate town hall meetings on relations between the U.S. and the Islamic world on more than a dozen college campuses across America. Believing that September 11 should be reserved as a day of mourning and commemoration, we chose September 12 for the town halls to symbolize a rise to action out of the ashes of tragedy. The "epicenter" town halls were in Washington, D.C. and New York City, in memory of the terrorist attacks in both cities, with "points of light" discussions occurring throughout the country. Janet Reno, six members of Congress, and seven ambassadors were among the many town hall participants.

The international solidarity that overtook the world on September 12, 2001 is a powerful symbol of what we can become. If America is ready to embrace the world, and the world is prepared to accept American involvement, we can together realize our common security and humanity. I am hopeful that my generation, through AID, town meetings, Interdependence Day programs and similar initiatives, can play a part in bringing the world back together, as it was in that fleeting moment after the attacks and from there more forward into an era of global cooperation and interdependence.

Published with permission of the author.

Part Three

How to Celebrate Interdependence Day— Every Year, Everywhere

Interdependence Day is everyone's celebration. It can only succeed if we take it upon ourselves to integrate the idea of interdependence into the way we think and act. Interdependence Day is a day for discussing the realities of interdependence, and making commitments to be responsible not only for ourselves and our local communities but for all the world's people.

Templates for Celebrations

Note: all templates are available for download from www.CivWorld.org

---

Celebrate Interdependence Day in Your School! Here's How!!

Please join us on Interdependence Day, September 12th, in reflecting on the realities of interdependence—and the civic responsibility that comes with it! Let's work together to create a new way—a new interdependent way of realizing the dream of "liberty and justice for all."

Help to create a new important tradition by celebrating Interdependence Day in your school every year on September 12th or, when it falls on a Saturday or Sunday, the following Monday. Use your imagination and creativity to make Interdependence Day a memorable occasion—informative and inspiring.

HERE ARE SOME SUGGESTIONS FOR GETTING IT OFF THE GROUND:

1. Form an Interdependence Day committee of faculty and students;

2. Request endorsements and proclamations from public officials, e.g. mayor, legislators, governors;

3. Have an assembly program featuring:

   - a public reading and signing of the Declaration of Interdependence;

   - a panel discussion on interdependence—what it means, its relationship to independence, how socio-political interdependence connects to interdependence in the natural environment, etc;

   - an appropriate artistic element: literature, music, theatre or dance;

   - a commitment to engage interdependently, e.g. in a virtual or actual student or faculty exchange, or volunteer with youth organizations in the community to conduct discussions on interdependence;

4. Assign readings on interdependence; conduct discussions in class. Suggested readings will be sent on request;

5. Sponsor an essay contest on interdependence using one of the readings as a text to which students can respond;

6. Make Interdependence Day an annual occasion in your school.

Why Interdependence Day?

We have launched Interdependence Day as an annual commemorative occasion for reflection on the reality of interdependence and its civic implications. In this post-communist, post-Cold War, post-9/11 era, Interdependence Day stands as a symbol of commitment to a more collaborative and humane future in which people throughout the world can enjoy the fruits of democracy-the promise of "liberty and justice for all."

Why you? Why me?

The success of this citizens' movement depends on all of us individuals and our institutions. Your celebrating Interdependence Day is a first step in choosing a future in which we expand our idea of citizenship to include not only our local communities and our nation but all the world's people. We are about people caring about and for people. Interdependence must be the guiding principle for civic life in the 21st century. It's up to us!

The CivWorld Citizens' Campaign for Democracy, a project of The Democracy Collaborative, at the University of Maryland includes three components:

• The Declaration of Interdependence
• Interdependence Day—September 12
• An Interdependence curriculum

For more information, contact:
Sondra Myers at (202) 496-5060
sondram@ix.netcom.com
Rainer Gude at (212) 247-5433
rgude@CivWorld.org
or
Visit our website: www.CivWorld.org

Celebrate Interdependence Day on Your Campus! Here's How!!

Please join us on Interdependence Day, September 12th, in reflecting on the realities of interdependence—and the civic responsibility that comes with it! Let's work together to create a new way—a new interdependent way of realizing the dream of "liberty and justice for all."

Help to create a new important tradition by celebrating Interdependence Day on your college or university campus every year on September 12th or, when it falls on a Saturday or Sunday, the following Monday. Use your imagination and creativity to make Interdependence Day a memorable occasion—informative and inspiring.

HERE ARE SOME SUGGESTIONS FOR GETTING IT OFF THE GROUND:

1. Form an Interdependence Day committee, enlisting administrators, faculty and students;

2. Request endorsements and proclamations from public officials, e.g. mayor, legislators, governors;

3. Recruit student government, civic, religious, social and international organizations into the project;

4. Hold a program featuring:

   • a public reading and signing of the Declaration of Interdependence;

   • a panel discussion on interdependence—what it means, its relationship to independence, how socio-political interdependence connects to interdependence in the natural environment, etc;

   • an appropriate artistic element: literature, music, theatre or dance;

   • a commitment to engage interdependently, e.g. in a virtual or actual student or faculty exchange, or volunteer with youth organizations in the community to conduct discussions on interdependence;

5. Conduct discussions in classes and extracurricular settings. Suggested readings will be sent on request.

6. Make Interdependence Day an annual occasion on your campus.

Why Interdependence Day?

We have launched Interdependence Day as an annual commemorative occasion for reflection on the reality of interdependence and its civic implications. In this post-communist, post-Cold War, post-9/11 era, Interdependence Day stands as a symbol of commitment to a more collaborative and humane future in which people throughout the world can enjoy the fruits of democracy-the promise of "liberty and justice for all."

Why you? Why me?

The success of this citizens' movement depends on all of us individuals and our institutions. Your celebrating Interdependence Day is a first step in choosing a future in which we expand our idea of citizenship to include not only our local communities and our nation but all the world's people. We are about people caring about and for people. Interdependence must be the guiding principle for civic life in the 21st century. It's up to us!

The CivWorld Citizens' Campaign for Democracy, a project of The Democracy Collaborative, at the University of Maryland includes three components:

• The Declaration of Interdependence

• Interdependence Day—September 12

• An Interdependence curriculum

For more information, contact:

Sondra Myers at (202) 496-5060
sondram@ix.netcom.com

Rainer Gude at (212) 247-5433
rgude@CivWorld.org

or

Visit our website: www.CivWorld.org

Celebrate Interdependence Day in Religious Institutions! Here's How!!

Please join us on Interdependence Day, September 12th, in reflecting on the realities of interdependence—and the civic responsibility that comes with it! Let's work together to create a new way—a new interdependent way of realizing the dream of "liberty and justice for all."

Help to create an important new tradition by celebrating Interdependence Day in your church, mosque, synagogue or temple every year on September 12th or the weekend closest to it. Your religious community, with its commitment to inspiring people to live with a sense of respect for and responsibility to each other, can assume leadership in teaching your members to pray, meditate, reflect, think and act according to the realities of interdependence. Make Interdependence Day a memorable occasion in your congregation!

HERE ARE SOME SUGGESTIONS FOR GETTING IT OFF THE GROUND:

1. Form an Interdependence Day committee comprising the spiritual leader, key members of the congregation and its young people;

2. Request endorsements and proclamations from public officials, e.g. mayor, legislators, governors;

3. Plan a sermon on Interdependence for the main service closest to September 12. Possible topics: "Who belongs in your moral universe?" or "Independence and Interdependence: In Conflict or on the Continuum?" or "Interdependence as a Guiding Principle" or an appropriate subject of choice. Suggested readings will be sent on request;

4. Include a public reading of the Declaration of Interdependence and an appropriate artistic selection;

5. Host an interfaith seminar on "Interdependence: Its Religious and Civic Implications in the 21st Century" or another appropriate topic;

6. Have congregation members, adults and youth, pledge to engage in some community activities which reflect interdependence in the coming year;

7. Make Interdependence Day an annual occasion in your congregation.

Why Interdependence Day?

We have launched Interdependence Day as an annual commemorative occasion for reflection on the reality of interdependence and its civic implications. In this post-communist, post-Cold War, post-9/11 era, Interdependence Day stands as a symbol of commitment to a more collaborative and humane future in which people throughout the world can enjoy the fruits of democracy-the promise of "liberty and justice for all."

Why you? Why me?

The success of this citizens' movement depends on all of us individuals and our institutions. Your celebrating Interdependence Day is a first step in choosing a future in which we expand our idea of citizenship to include not only our local communities and our nation but all the world's people. We are about people caring about and for people. Interdependence must be the guiding principle for civic life in the 21st century. It's up to us!

The CivWorld Citizens' Campaign for Democracy, a project of The Democracy Collaborative, at the University of Maryland includes three components:

• The Declaration of Interdependence
• Interdependence Day—September 12
• An Interdependence curriculum

For more information, contact:
Sondra Myers at (202) 496-5060
sondram@ix.netcom.com
Rainer Gude at (212) 247-5433
rgude@CivWorld.org
or
Visit our website: www.CivWorld.org

Celebrate Interdependence Day in Civic and Cultural Institutions! Here's How!!

Please join us on Interdependence Day, September 12th, in reflecting on the realities of interdependence—and the civic responsibility that comes with it! Let's work together to create a new way—a new interdependent way of realizing the dream of "liberty and justice for all."

Help to create an important new tradition by celebrating Interdependence Day in your service club, social service organization, museum or library every year on September 12th. Non-profit organizations, with their special commitment to making life better for all individuals and for the community at large, can assume leadership in teaching people to think and act according to the realities of interdependence. Make Interdependence Day a memorable occasion in your organization!

HERE ARE SOME SUGGESTIONS FOR GETTING IT OFF THE GROUND:

1. Form an Interdependence Day planning committee within your organization, comprising staff, board and constituents, including young people;

2. Request endorsements and proclamations from public officials, e.g. mayor, legislators, governors;

3. Plan a program, e.g. a discussion based on designated texts about the need to acknowledge the realities of interdependence in today's world. It might focus on "Who is in our moral universe?" or "Independence and Interdependence: In Conflict or on the Continuum?" or "Interdependence as a Guiding Principle for the 21st Century" or an appropriate subject of choice. Texts suggested on request;

4. Include a public reading of the Declaration of Interdependence and an appropriate artistic selection;

5. Alert the media to the Interdependence Day event and seek their coverage;

6. Have members, adults and youth, pledge to engage in some community activities which reflect interdependence in the coming year;

7. Make interdependence an annual occasion in your organization.

Why Interdependence Day?

We have launched Interdependence Day as an annual commemorative occasion for reflection on the reality of interdependence and its civic implications. In this post-communist, post-Cold War, post-9/11 era, Interdependence Day stands as a symbol of commitment to a more collaborative and humane future in which people throughout the world can enjoy the fruits of democracy-the promise of "liberty and justice for all."

Why you? Why me?

The success of this citizens' movement depends on all of us individuals and our institutions. Your celebrating Interdependence Day is a first step in choosing a future in which we expand our idea of citizenship to include not only our local communities and our nation but all the world's people. We are about people caring about and for people. Interdependence must be the guiding principle for civic life in the 21st century. It's up to us!

The CivWorld Citizens' Campaign for Democracy, a project of The Democracy Collaborative, at the University of Maryland includes three components:

• The Declaration of Interdependence
• Interdependence Day—September 12
• An Interdependence curriculum

For more information, contact:
Sondra Myers at (202) 496-5060
sondram@ix.netcom.com
Rainer Gude at (212) 247-5433
rgude@CivWorld.org
or
Visit our website: www.CivWorld.org

Celebrate Interdependence Day as a Community! Here's How!!

Please join us on Interdependence Day, September 12th, in reflecting on the realities of interdependence—and the civic responsibility that comes with it! Let's work together to create a new way—a new interdependent way of realizing the dream of "liberty and justice for all."

Interdependence is at the very core of community. By bringing educational, religious, civic and cultural leaders together in your community to celebrate Interdependence Day in their various institutions on September 12 (and/or September 11 and 13) in creative and inspiring ways, you will advance and expand the idea of community to include not just the local and national, but the global! It's an important step for us all in the 21st century.

HERE ARE SOME SUGGESTIONS FOR GETTING IT OFF THE GROUND:

1. Convene an Interdependence Day committee including representatives of the school district, local colleges and universities, media leaders, religious leaders, civic and cultural activists, etc. to discuss a joint kickoff event and events in their respective institutions;

2. Request endorsements and proclamations by public officials, mayors, county commissioners, legislators, governors;

3. Work with media to get the word out!

4. Hold a kickoff event featuring:

   a. A public reading of the Declaration of Interdependence

   b. A keynote speaker or panel discussion on interdependence—what it means, its relationship to independence, how socio-political, civic interdependence relates to interdependence in the natural environment, etc.

   c. An appropriate artistic element—literature, music, theater or dance;

   d. A commitment to engage interdependently on a regular basis, both within the community and with a community or communities in another part of the world.

Why Interdependence Day?

We have launched Interdependence Day as an annual commemorative occasion for reflection on the reality of interdependence and its civic implications. In this post-communist, post-Cold War, post-9/11 era, Interdependence Day stands as a symbol of commitment to a more collaborative and humane future in which people throughout the world can enjoy the fruits of democracy-the promise of "liberty and justice for all."

Why you? Why me?

The success of this citizens' movement depends on all of us individuals and our institutions. Your celebrating Interdependence Day is a first step in choosing a future in which we expand our idea of citizenship to include not only our local communities and our nation but all the world's people. We are about people caring about and for people. Interdependence must be the guiding principle for civic life in the 21st century. It's up to us!

The CivWorld Citizens' Campaign for Democracy, a project of The Democracy Collaborative, at the University of Maryland includes three components:

• The Declaration of Interdependence
• Interdependence Day—September 12
• An Interdependence curriculum

For more information, contact:

Sondra Myers at (202) 496-5060
sondram@ix.netcom.com
Rainer Gude at (212) 247-5433
rgude@CivWorld.org
or
Visit our website: www.CivWorld.org

Interdependence at a Glance

An Index of Interesting Interdependence Facts
Compiled by Joshua Karant

BANNING LANDMINES   In 1991 both non-governmental organizations and individuals began the movement to ban antipersonnel landmines. The International Campaign to Ban Landmines (ICBL) was formalized a year later. As of May 13, 2004, the ICBL has 151 signatories and 142 ratifications. As of the same date, 43 countries have *not* signed the treaty including the United States, Iraq, Iran, China, Cuba, Egypt, Somalia, Russia, Libya, Lebanon, Sri Lanka, the United Arab Emirates, Russia, Saudi Arabia, and North Korea.

DNA

- Human beings share 98% of their DNA sequences with chimpanzees. Many genes present in humans are also present in mice, fish, fruit flies, yeast, and bacteria.

- On average, two random people share the same DNA sequence in 99.9% of their genome, and differ in only one of every thousand nucleotides.

FAST FOOD   McDonald's has restaurants in 121 countries around the world, on every continent but Antartica. While menu items are standard, the company also develops dishes which appeal to the host country's cultural preferences. Examples include rice dishes in Japan, beer in Germany, Kiwiburgers in New Zealand, McSpaghetti in the Philippines, Samurai Porkburgers in Thailand, and Uruguay's "McHuevo"—a hamburger topped with a poached egg.

GLOBAL CITIES   The top ten "Global Cities" of 2003—measured by the number of their international non-governmental organizations and transnational corporations—are Frankfurt, Hong Kong, London, Madrid, Milan, New York, Paris, Singapore, Sydney, and Tokyo.

GLOBAL TOURISM   The number of global tourists has increased 52% between 1990 and 2000. The sharpest increase has been in travel to low and middle income regions. Tourism to low income regions has increased 99%, while tourism to middle income regions has increased by 68%.

INFORMATION TECHNOLOGY The boom in information technology is linking peoples around the world. Cable television subscribers have increased 48% between 1995 and 2000; between 1991 and 2001, the average number of telephone lines increased 80% in low and middle income regions, and 43% in high income regions; the average number of mobile telephone subscribers increased 504% worldwide between 1995 and 2001; and an estimated 1 out of every 125 people are internet users.

INTERNATIONAL COLLABORATION International organizations are growing increasingly interdependent. Between 1992 and 2002 there was a 60% increase in the number of non-governmental organizations and international governmental organizations established in collaboration with another group. Similarly, there was a 74% increase in groups with structural links to other organizations; a 261% increase in financial ties between organizations, a 52% increase in joint activities, and a 130% increase in membership links between organizations.

MOVIES The film "American Pie 3: American Wedding" (2003) was a co-production of the U.S and Germany, grossing $104 million in the U.S. and $123 million overseas. If you were to see the film at a Loews Cinema in Manhattan, your ticket-seller might be from the Dominican Republic, China, or Jamaica—the three largest foreign-born populations in New York which, together, comprise over 20% of the city's total population. Loews Cineplex Corporation also has theaters in Mexico, Spain, Canada, and Korea, and is jointly owned by the Canadian conglomerate Onex and American company Oaktree.

POPULATIONS ON THE MOVE
- According to the United Nations, at least 185 million people worldwide currently live outside their countries of birth, an increase of over 100 million in thirty years. Nearly one of every 275 people on the planet is a refugee—either in exile, returned, or internally displaced—for a total of 21.7 million. The International Organization for Migration estimates that criminal organizations "traffic" approximately 4 million people per year into the sex trade and other exploitative global trades for over $7 billion in profits. Approximately 50,000 annually—the majority of whom are women and children—are trafficked to the United States for illicit purposes. Approximately 3% of the world's people live outside their country of birth. The largest migrant populations are those of Europe (54 million), Asia (41 million), North America (40 million), and Africa (13 million).
- Nearly one-quarter of Jordan's Gross Domestic Product (GDP) comes from money sent home by workers who have moved to other countries. Migrant workers

abroad also contribute between 11% and 15% of the GDP of Yemen, Albania, Bosnia-Herzegovina, El Salvador, Nicaragua, and Jamaica.

POVERTY AND DISEASE

- Half the world is living on less than $2 a day.

- One billion people live on less than a dollar a day and go to bed hungry every night.

- 1.5 billion people don't get a single clean glass of water in their lives.

- 10 million children die every year of completely preventable childhood diseases.

- One in four of all the people who will die this year will die of AIDS, TB, malaria and infections related to diarrhea, most of them young children.

- 130 million children never attend school at all.

SPORTS

- 28 of the 29 sports teams in the National Basketball Association (NBA) have international players—a total of 67 from 33 countries and territories. This group includes two-time Most Valuable Player Tim Duncan (U.S. Virgin Islands), and 2004 All-Stars from Russia, Canada, Germany, China, Serbia and Montenegro. The team with the largest number of international players (7 of 12)—the San Antonio Spurs—has won two NBA Championships since 1999. In recognition of its growing international fan base, the NBA has also begun a Basketball Without Borders program. Camp programs for youth promoting friendship, healthy living and education, as well as basketball, will be held in 2004, in Rio de Janeiro, Brazil, Treviso, Italy, and Johannesburg, South Africa.

- In total and throughout the globe, the 2002 World Cup for soccer was broadcast for 41,000 hours. Competing teams came from 32 countries and 5 continents. Following suit, Major League Baseball is currently exploring the possibility of a world tournament for the spring of 2005, involving teams from 16 countries.

TRANSNATIONAL CORPORATIONS INCREASE

- Transnational corporations (TNCs) demonstrate the increasing financial strength of global markets. The average annual amount invested by nations quadrupled in the 1990s. Foreign assets of the top 100 TNCs totaled nearly $2.5 billion in 2000; in that year, General Motors was worth more than the national economy of New Zealand.

- America's most visible corporations make their largest profits overseas: 62% of Coca Cola's, 59.2% of McDonald's, 69.4% of ExxonMobil's, and 57.9% of IBM's sales are foreign.

- Of the more than 500,000 factory workers employed by Nike in 2001, more than half were Chinese and Indonesian.

- In low and middle income regions of the world, trade has risen at least 44% between 1990 and 2000. As of 2000, 45.8% of the World's GDP is earned through trade.

TRAVELING ARMS   Arms left by American soldiers in Vietnam in the early 1970s were shipped from Ho Chi Minh City to Singapore to Bremerhaven, Germany through the Panama Canal, to Long Beach, California and then to Mexico when, in March, 1997, they were discovered and seized by federal agents on the US-Mexico border.

WEST NILE VIRUS   West Nile Virus was first identified in 1937 in Uganda. Since then, it has spread throughout the Middle East and central and southern Europe to Morocco (through horses), to Israel (through geese flocks), and the United States (through a traveler bitten by an infected mosquito). Cases have recently been discovered in the Cayman Islands and Mexico, and are expected in South America.

Part Four

Historical Documents

Declaration of Interdependence

September 12, 2003

We the people of the world do herewith declare our interdependence as individuals and members of distinct communities and nations. We do pledge ourselves citizens of one CivWorld, civic, civil and civilized. Without prejudice to the goods and interests of our national and regional identities, we recognize our responsibilities to the common goods and liberties of humankind as a whole.

We do therefore pledge to work both directly and through the nations and communities of which we are also citizens:

TO GUARANTEE justice and equality for all by establishing on a firm basis the human rights of every person on the planet, ensuring that the least among us may enjoy the same liberties as the prominent and the powerful;

TO FORGE a safe and sustainable global environment for all—which is the condition of human survival—at a cost to peoples based on their current share in the world's wealth;

TO OFFER children, our common human future, special attention and protection in distributing our common goods, above all those upon which health and education depend;

TO ESTABLISH democratic forms of global, civil, and legal governance through which our common rights can be secured and our common ends realized;

TO FOSTER democratic policies and institutions expressing and protecting our human commonality; and at the same time,

TO NURTURE free spaces in which our distinctive religious, ethnic and cultural identities may flourish and our equally worthy lives may be lived in dignity, protected from political, economic and cultural hegemony of every kind.

Signature _____

Name _____

Affiliation_____

Address _____

Nationality _____

Email_____ Tel/Fax_____

Please sign and return via fax (212-247-5413) or mail:
The Democracy Collaborative, 1841 Broadway, Suite 1008, New York, NY 10023.
www.civworld.org

Millennium Development Goals

In September 2000, at the United Nations Millennium Summit, world leaders agreed to a set of time-bound and measurable goals and targets for combating poverty, hunger, disease, illiteracy, environmental degradation and discrimination against women. Placed at the heart of the global agenda, they are now called the Millennium Development Goals (MDGs). The Summit's Millennium Declaration also outlined a consensus "road map" for how to proceed, with a stronger focus on human rights, good governance and democracy.

At the International Conference on Financing for Development at Monterrey, Mexico in 2002, leaders from both developed and developing countries started to match these commitments with resources and action, signalling a global deal in which sustained political and economic reform by developing countries will be matched by direct support from the developed world in the form of aid, trade, debt relief and investment.

The MDGs provide a framework for the entire UN system to work coherently together toward a common end. Partnered with the rest of the UN Development Group (UNDG), the UN Development Programme (UNDP)'s global development network is at the centre of those efforts. On the ground in virtually every developing country, UNDP is uniquely positioned to advocate for change, connect countries to knowledge and resources, and help coordinate broader UN efforts at the country level.

The world is making progress toward the MDGs—but it is uneven and too slow. A large majority of nations will reach the MDGs only if they get substantial support—advocacy, expertise and resources—from outside. The challenges for the global community, in both the developed and developing world, are to mobilize financial support and political will, re-engage governments, reorient development priorities and policies, build capacity and reach out to partners in civil society and the private sector.

MILLENNIUM DEVELOPMENT GOALS TO BE ACHIEVED BY 2015

- **Halve extreme poverty and hunger**   1.2 billion people still live on less than US$1 a day. But 43 countries, with more than 60 percent of the world's people, have already met or are on track to meet the goal of cutting hunger in half by 2015.

- **Achieve universal primary education**   113 million children do not attend school, but this goal is within reach; India, for example, should have 95 percent of its children in school by 2005.

- **Empower women and promote equality between women and men**   Two-thirds of the world's illiterates are women, and 80 percent of its refugees are women and children. Since the 1997 Microcredit Summit, progress has been made reaching and empowering nearly 19 million poor women in 2000 alone.

- **Reduce under-five mortality by two-thirds**   11 million young children die every year;but that number is down from 15 million in 1980.

- **Reduce maternal mortality by three-quarters**   In the developing world, the risk of dying in childbirth is one in 48. But virtually all countries now have safe motherhood programmes and are poised for progress.

- **Reverse the spread of killer diseases, especially HIV/AIDS and malaria**   Diseases that have erased a generation of development gains. Countries like Brazil, Senegal, Thailand and Uganda have shown that we can stop HIV in its tracks.

- **Ensure environmental sustainability**   More than one billion people still lack access to safe drinking water; however, during the 1990s, nearly one billion people gained access to safe water and as many to sanitation.

- **Create a global partnership for development, with targets for aid, trade and debt relief**   Too many developing countries are spending more on debt service than on social services. New aid commitments made in the first half of 2002 alone, though, will reach an additional $12 billion per year by 2006.

FOR FURTHER INFORMATION CONTACT YOUR LOCAL UNDP OFFICE OR:
United Nations Development Programme
One United Nations Plaza
New York,NY 10017
USA
Telephone: (212) 906 5295 Fax: (212) 906 5364

Programme des Nations Unies pour le développement
Bureau européen
Palais des Nations
CH-1211 Genève 10
Switzerland
Telephone: (41-22) 917 8542 Fax: (41-22) 917 8001
UNDP Liaison Office in Brussels

United Nations Office/UNDP
14 Rue Montoyer
1000 - Bruxelles Belgium
Telephone: (32-2) 505 4620 Fax: (32-2) 503 4729

UNDP Nordic Office
Midtermolen 3, PO Box 2530
DK-2100
København Ø
Denmark
Telephone: (45-35) 46 71 54 Fax: (45-35) 46 70 95

UNDP Tokyo Office
UNU Building, 8th Floor
5-53-70 Jingumae
Shibuya-ku, Tokyo 150-0001
Japan
Telephone: (813) 5467 4751 Fax: (813) 5467 4753

UNDP Liaison Office in Washington, DC
1775 K Street, NW, Suite 420
Washington, DC 20006
USA
Telephone: (202) 331 9130 Fax: (202) 331 9363

For more information, visit: www.undp.org

Preamble to A Call to Our Guiding Institutions

*Council for a Parliament of The World's Religions
Capetown, South Africa 1999*

As human beings

   . . . we are all interdependent and must relate to each other respectfully and peacefully;

   . . . we are all—children, women, men—worthy of a meaningful life, and must treat all others with fairness, kindness, encouragement, and love;

   . . . we are all responsible for the care of the Earth on which we depend and the well-being of the communities in which we live;

   . . . we know that our individual and collective futures will be reshaped by the extent to which we link our societies in partnerships that reach across the continents and across racial, ethnic, cultural, sexual, social, political, economic, and religious lines.

As religious and spiritual persons

> . . . we center our lives in an Ultimate Reality, which our traditions call by various names (the Absolute, Allah, Brahman, Dharmakaya, God, Great Spirit, the One, Waheguru), drawing hope and strength therefrom, in trust and vision, in word and silence, in service and solidarity;

> . . . we seek to foster creative engagement among the guiding institutions that so profoundly influence life on Earth, in order that they may find imaginative new ways to address the critical issues that confront us all.

As members of the Earth community

> . . . we affirm the keystone principle of the document Towards a Global Ethic: An Initial Declaration:

>> Every human being must be treated humanely!

> We further affirm the four commitments ensuing from this principle:

>> • Commitment to a Culture of Non-Violence and Respect for Life,
>>
>> • Commitment to a Culture of Solidarity and a Just Economic Order,
>>
>> • Commitment to a Culture of Tolerance and a Life of Truthfulness,
>>
>> • Commitment to a Culture of Equal Rights and Partnership between Men and Women.

Together, on the occasion of the 1999 Parliament of the World's Religions in Cape Town, we extend this *Call* to these guiding institutions whose decisions and actions will mean so much to the future of the entire community of the Earth, urging each to reassess and redefine its role for a new century toward the realization of a just, peaceful, and sustainable future.

Earth Charter
Earth Charter Initiative
2000

PREAMBLE

We stand at a critical moment in Earth's history, a time when humanity must choose its future. As the world becomes increasingly interdependent and fragile, the future at once holds great peril and great promise. To move forward we must recognize that in the midst of a magnificent diversity of cultures and life forms we are one human family and one Earth community with a common destiny. We must join together to bring forth a sustainable global society founded on respect for nature, universal human rights, economic justice, and a culture of peace. Towards this end, it is imperative that we, the peoples of Earth, declare our responsibility to one another, to the greater community of life, and to future generations.

Earth, Our Home

Humanity is part of a vast evolving universe. Earth, our home, is alive with a unique community of life. The forces of nature make existence a demanding and uncertain adventure, but Earth has provided the conditions essential to life's evolution. The resilience of the community of life and the well-being of humanity depend upon preserving a healthy biosphere with all its ecological systems, a rich variety of plants and animals, fertile soils, pure waters, and clean air. The global environment with its finite resources is a common concern of all peoples. The protection of Earth's vitality, diversity, and beauty is a sacred trust.

The Global Situation

The dominant patterns of production and consumption are causing environmental devastation, the depletion of resources, and a massive extinction of species. Communities are being undermined. The benefits of development are not shared equitably and the gap between rich and poor is widening. Injustice, poverty, ignorance, and violent conflict are widespread and the cause of great suffering. An unprecedented rise in human population has overburdened ecological and social systems. The foundations of global security are threatened. These trends are perilous—but not inevitable.

The Challenges Ahead

The choice is ours: form a global partnership to care for Earth and one another or risk the destruction of ourselves and the diversity of life. Fundamental changes are needed in our values, institutions, and ways of living. We must realize that when basic needs have been met, human development is primarily about being more, not having more. We have the knowledge and technology to provide for all and to reduce our impacts on the environment. The emergence of a global civil society is creating new opportunities to build a democratic and humane world. Our environmental, economic, political, social, and spiritual challenges are interconnected, and together we can forge inclusive solutions.

Universal Responsibility

To realize these aspirations, we must decide to live with a sense of universal responsibility, identifying ourselves with the whole Earth community as well as our local communities. We are at once citizens of different nations and of one world in which the local and global are linked. Everyone shares responsibility for the present and future well-being of the human family and the larger living world. The spirit of human solidarity and kinship with all life is strengthened when we live with reverence for the mystery of being, gratitude for the gift of life, and humility regarding the human place in nature.

We urgently need a shared vision of basic values to provide an ethical foundation for the emerging world community. Therefore, together in hope we affirm the following interdependent principles for a sustainable way of life as a common standard by which the conduct of all individuals, organizations, businesses, governments, and transnational institutions is to be guided
and assessed.

PRINCIPLES

I. Respect and Care for the Community of Life

1. Respect Earth and life in all its diversity.

    a. Recognize that all beings are interdependent and every form of life has value regardless of its worth to human beings.

    b. Affirm faith in the inherent dignity of all human beings and in the intellectual, artistic, ethical, and spiritual potential of humanity.

2. Care for the community of life with understanding, compassion, and love.

    a. Accept that with the right to own, manage, and use natural resources comes the duty to prevent environmental harm and to protect the rights of people.

    b. Affirm that with increased freedom, knowledge, and power comes increased responsibility to promote the common good.

3. Build democratic societies that are just, participatory, sustainable, and peaceful.

    a. Ensure that communities at all levels guarantee human rights and fundamental freedoms and provide everyone an opportunity to realize his or her full potential.

  b. Promote social and economic justice, enabling all to achieve a secure and meaningful livelihood that is ecologically responsible.

 4. Secure Earth's bounty and beauty for present and future generations.

  a. Recognize that the freedom of action of each generation is qualified by the needs of future generations.

  b. Transmit to future generations values, traditions, and institutions that support the long-term flourishing of Earth's human and ecological communities. In order to fulfill these four broad commitments, it is necessary to:

II. Ecological Integrity

 5. Protect and restore the integrity of Earth's ecological systems, with special concern for biological diversity and the natural processes that sustain life.

  a. Adopt at all levels sustainable development plans and regulations that make environmental conservation and rehabilitation integral to all development initiatives.

  b. Establish and safeguard viable nature and biosphere reserves, including wild lands and marine areas, to protect Earth's life support systems, maintain biodiversity, and preserve our natural heritage.

  c. Promote the recovery of endangered species and ecosystems.

  d. Control and eradicate non-native or genetically modified organisms harmful to native species and the environment, and prevent introduction of such harmful organisms.

  e. Manage the use of renewable resources such as water, soil, forest products, and marine life in ways that do not exceed rates of regeneration and that protect the health of ecosystems.

  f. Manage the extraction and use of non-renewable resources such as minerals and fossil fuels in ways that minimize depletion and cause no serious environmental damage.

 6. Prevent harm as the best method of environmental protection and, when knowledge is limited, apply a precautionary approach.

  a. Take action to avoid the possibility of serious or irreversible environmental harm even when scientific knowledge is incomplete or inconclusive.

  b. Place the burden of proof on those who argue that a proposed activity will not cause significant harm, and make the responsible parties liable for environmental harm.

    c. Ensure that decision making addresses the cumulative, long-term, indirect, long distance, and global consequences of human activities.

    d. Prevent pollution of any part of the environment and allow no build-up of radioactive, toxic, or other hazardous substances.

    e. Avoid military activities damaging to the environment.

7. Adopt patterns of production, consumption, and reproduction that safeguard Earth's regenerative capacities, human rights, and community well-being.

    a. Reduce, reuse, and recycle the materials used in production and consumption systems, and ensure that residual waste can be assimilated by ecological systems.

    b. Act with restraint and efficiency when using energy, and rely increasingly on renewable energy sources such as solar and wind.

    c. Promote the development, adoption, and equitable transfer of environmentally sound technologies.

    d. Internalize the full environmental and social costs of goods and services in the selling price, and enable consumers to identify products that meet the highest social and environmental standards.

    e. Ensure universal access to health care that fosters reproductive health and responsible reproduction.

    f. Adopt lifestyles that emphasize the quality of life and material sufficiency in a finite world.

8. Advance the study of ecological sustainability and promote the open exchange and wide application of the knowledge acquired.

    a. Support international scientific and technical cooperation on sustainability, with special attention to the needs of developing nations.

    b. Recognize and preserve the traditional knowledge and spiritual wisdom in all cultures that contribute to environmental protection and human well-being.

    c. Ensure that information of vital importance to human health and environmental protection, including genetic information, remains available in the public domain.

III. Social and Economic Justice

9. Eradicate poverty as an ethical, social, and environmental imperative.

    a. Guarantee the right to potable water, clean air, food security, uncontaminated soil, shelter, and safe sanitation, allocating the national and international resources required.

b. Empower every human being with the education and resources to secure a sustainable livelihood, and provide social security and safety nets for those who are unable to support themselves.

c. Recognize the ignored, protect the vulnerable, serve those who suffer, and enable them to develop their capacities and to pursue their aspirations.

10. Ensure that economic activities and institutions at all levels promote human development in an equitable and sustainable manner.

a. Promote the equitable distribution of wealth within nations and among nations.

b. Enhance the intellectual, financial, technical, and social resources of developing nations, and relieve them of onerous international debt.

c. Ensure that all trade supports sustainable resource use, environmental protection, and progressive labor standards.

d. Require multinational corporations and international financial organizations to act transparently in the public good, and hold them accountable for the consequences of their activities.

11. Affirm gender equality and equity as prerequisites to sustainable development and ensure universal access to education, health care, and economic opportunity.

a. Secure the human rights of women and girls and end all violence against them.

b. Promote the active participation of women in all aspects of economic, political, civil, social, and cultural life as full and equal partners, decision makers, leaders, and beneficiaries.

c. Strengthen families and ensure the safety and loving nurture of all family members.

12. Uphold the right of all, without discrimination, to a natural and social environment supportive of human dignity, bodily health, and spiritual wellbeing, with special attention to the rights of indigenous peoples and minorities.

a. Eliminate discrimination in all its forms, such as that based on race, color, sex, sexual orientation, religion, language, and national, ethnic or social origin.

b. Affirm the right of indigenous peoples to their spirituality, knowledge, lands and resources and to their related practice of sustainable livelihoods.

    c. Honor and support the young people of our communities, enabling them to fulfill their essential role in creating sustainable societies.

    d. Protect and restore outstanding places of cultural and spiritual significance.

IV. Democracy, Nonviolence, and Peace

13. Strengthen democratic institutions at all levels, and provide transparency and accountability in governance, inclusive participation in decision making, and access to justice.

    a. Uphold the right of everyone to receive clear and timely information on environmental matters and all development plans and activities which are likely to affect them or in which they have an interest.

    b. Support local, regional and global civil society, and promote the meaningful participation of all interested individuals and organizations in decision making.

    c. Protect the rights to freedom of opinion, expression, peaceful assembly, association, and dissent.

    d. Institute effective and efficient access to administrative and independent judicial procedures, including remedies and redress for environmental harm and the threat of such harm.

    e. Eliminate corruption in all public and private institutions.

    f. Strengthen local communities, enabling them to care for their environments, and assign environmental responsibilities to the levels of government where they can be carried out most effectively.

14. Integrate into formal education and life-long learning the knowledge, values, and skills needed for a sustainable way of life.

    a. Provide all, especially children and youth, with educational opportunities that empower them to contribute actively to sustainable development.

    b. Promote the contribution of the arts and humanities as well as the sciences in sustainability education.

    c. Enhance the role of the mass media in raising awareness of ecological and social challenges.

    d. Recognize the importance of moral and spiritual education for sustainable living.

15. Treat all living beings with respect and consideration.

    a. Prevent cruelty to animals kept in human societies and protect them from suffering.

    b. Protect wild animals from methods of hunting, trapping, and fishing that cause extreme, prolonged, or avoidable suffering.

    c. Avoid or eliminate to the full extent possible the taking or destruction of non-targeted species.

16. Promote a culture of tolerance, nonviolence, and peace.

    a. Encourage and support mutual understanding, solidarity, and cooperation among all peoples and within and among nations.

    b. Implement comprehensive strategies to prevent violent conflict and use collaborative problem solving to manage and resolve environmental conflicts and other disputes.

    c. Demilitarize national security systems to the level of a non-provocative defense posture, and convert military resources to peaceful purposes, including ecological restoration.

    d. Eliminate nuclear, biological, and toxic weapons and other weapons of mass destruction.

    e. Ensure that the use of orbital and outer space supports environmental protection and peace.

    f. Recognize that peace is the wholeness created by right relationships with oneself, other persons, other cultures, other life, Earth, and the larger whole of which all are a part.

THE WAY FORWARD

As never before in history, common destiny beckons us to seek a new beginning. Such renewal is the promise of these Earth Charter principles. To fulfill this promise, we must commit ourselves to adopt and promote the values and objectives of the Charter.

This requires a change of mind and heart. It requires a new sense of global interdependence and universal responsibility. We must imaginatively develop and apply the vision of a sustainable way of life locally, nationally, regionally, and globally. Our cultural diversity is a precious heritage and different cultures will find their own distinctive ways to realize the vision. We must deepen and expand the global dialogue that generated the Earth Charter, for we have much to learn from the ongoing collaborative search for truth and wisdom.

Life often involves tensions between important values. This can mean difficult choices. However, we must find ways to harmonize diversity with unity, the exercise of freedom with the common good, short term objectives with long term goals. Every individual, family, organization, and community has a vital role to play. The arts, sciences, religions, educational institutions, media, businesses, nongovernmental organizations, and governments are all called to offer creative leadership. The partnership of government, civil society, and business is essential for effective governance.

In order to build a sustainable global community, the nations of the world must renew their commitment to the United Nations, fulfill their obligations under existing international agreements, and support the implementation of Earth Charter principles with an international legally binding instrument on environment and development.

Let ours be a time remembered for the awakening of a new reverence for life, the firm resolve to achieve sustainability, the quickening of the struggle for justice and peace, and the joyful celebration of life.

EARTH CHARTER COMMISSION
Africa and the Middle East
Amadou Toumani Touré, Mali*
Princess Basma Bint Talal, Jordan
Wangari Maathai, Kenya
Mohamed Sahnoun, Algeria

Asia and the Pacific
Kamla Chowdhry, India*
A.T. Ariyaratne, Sri Lanka
Wakako Hironaka, Japan
Pauline Tangiora, New Zealand/Aoteroa
Erna Witoelar, Indonesia

Europe
Mikhail Gorbachev, Russia*
Pierre Calame, France
Ruud Lubbers, The Netherlands
Federico Mayor, Spain
Henriette Rasmussen, Greenland
Awraham Soetendorp, The Netherlands

North America
Maurice F. Strong, Canada*
John Hoyt, United States of America
Elizabeth May, Canada
Steven Rockefeller, United States of America
Severn Cullis-Suzuki, Canada

Latin America and the Caribbean
Mercedes Sosa, Argentina*
Leonardo Boff, Brazil
Yolanda Kakabadse, Ecuador
Shridath Ramphal, Guyana
Co-chair

STEERING COMMITTEE
Co-chairs
Kamla Chowdhry, India
Yolanda Kakabadse, Ecuador
Ruud Lubbers, The Netherlands
Steven Rockefeller, United States of America

Wakako Hironaka, Japan
Alexander Likhotal, Russia
Wangari Maathai, Kenya
Mohamed Sahnoun, Algeria
Severn Cullis-Suzuki, Canada
Rick Clugston, United States of America*
Chair, Finance Committee

Maximo Kalaw, Philippines
In Memoriam

For more information please contact:
Mirian Vilela, Executive Director
Earth Charter International Secretariat
c/o University for Peace
P.O. Box 319-6100 San José, Costa Rica
Phone: (506) 205-1600
Fax: (506) 249-3500
E-mail: info@earthcharter.org
Website: http://www.earthcharter.org

Interfaith Declaration

Rabbis for Human Rights

We, Muslim, Jewish, Christian and Druze religious leaders, cry out in the name of our One God to recognize one another, all created in God's image. Hate is boundless not only in the Middle East but also around the globe. We must look into our religious traditions and speak out in the name of compassion and justice. Our task as religious leaders is to engage our own people in self-reflection and point the way to a better future for our children and ourselves.

We, therefore, out of our respective religious traditions

- Condemn all acts of violence and human rights violations, seeing as they contradict God's will for humanity. The suffering of Palestinians and Israelis must stop. An attack against any human being is an attack against God.

- Call upon Israelis and Palestinians to recognize each other's humanity, deep roots in this land and suffering. We must find the courage to break the cycle of violence and human rights violations. Each act of violence being committed by either side elicits further violence.

- Call for energizing the vision of peace through negotiations, based on international legitimacy and respect for international law and the shared ethics of our religious traditions, thus fulfilling the national aspirations of two peoples and ensuring the human right to live free from occupation and fear.

- Welcome the Saudi proposal. Emanating from Mecca, the heart of Islam, these principles can potentially serve as a basis for feeing us all from the occupation, cycle of violence, human rights violations and pervasive insecurity that impede the realization of peace. We also welcome the Alexandria Declaration

- Draw from the wisdom of our faiths to accept the particularity of each of our traditions while respecting one's right to be different. Our Houses of worship must remain open and unharmed with free access for all, especially in Jerusalem. Any desecration of our sanctuaries and cemeteries is a desecration of God's presence in this world. Even more important than those sanctuaries built of stone are the sanctuaries which God has implanted within each and every human being.

- Agree to act as a living bridge between despair and hope and re-ignite the peace process, acting as mediators where possible and as agents of faith and instruments of love where it seems impossible. We will collectively and individually employ all of our influence in every conceivable way to realize a vision which goes beyond the cessation of hostilities and looks forward to the day when our peoples will be a mutual blessing to each other. We will meet among ourselves and engage our peoples and leaders.

In the name of God Who is compassionate and just, in the Name of God Who hears the cries of all those who suffer, in the name of God Who demands that we pursue justice through just means and seek peace by actively pursuing it, we call on the peoples and leaders of the Middle East and the world to act at once.

☾

A Declaration of INTERdependence

Henry Steele Commager
October 24, 1975

IN THE COURSE OF HISTORY the threat of extinction confronts mankind, it is necessary for the people of The United States to declare their interdependence with the people of and nations and to embrace those principles and build those institutions which will enable mankind to survive and civilization to flourish.

TWO CENTURIES AGO our forefathers brought forth a new nation; now we must join with others to bring forth a new world order. On this historic occasion it is proper that the American people should reaffirm those principles on which the United States of America was founded, acknowledge the new crises which confront them, accept the new obligations which history imposes upon them, and set forth the causes which impel them to affirm before all peoples their commitment to a Declaration of Interdependence.

WE HOLD THESE TRUTHS TO BE SELF-EVIDENT: that all men are created equal; that the inequalities and injustices which afflict so much of the human race are the product of history and society, not of God and nature; that people everywhere are entitled to the blessings of life and liberty, peace and security and the realization of their full potential; that they have an inescapable moral obligation to preserve those rights for posterity; and that to achieve these ends all the peoples and nations of the globe should acknowledge their interdependence and join together to dedicate their minds and their hearts to the solution of those problems which threaten their survival.

TO ESTABLISH A NEW WORLD ORDER of compassion, peace, justice and security, it is essential that mankind free itself from the limitations of national prejudice, and acknowledge that the forces that unite it are incomparably deeper than those that divide it—that all people are part of one global community, dependent on one body of resources, bound together by the ties of a common humanity and associated in a common adventure on the planet Earth.

LET US THEN JOIN TOGETHER to vindicate and realize this great truth that mankind is one, and as one will nobly save or irreparably lose the heritage of thousands of years of civilization. And let us set forth the principles which should animate and inspire us if our civilization is to survive.

WE AFFIRM that the resources of the globe are finite, not infinite, that they are the heritage of no one nation or generation, but of all peoples, nations and of posterity, and that our deepest obligation is to transmit to that posterity a planet richer in material bounty, in beauty and in delight that we found it. Narrow notions of national sovereignty must not be permitted to curtail that obligation.

WE AFFIRM that the exploitation of the poor by the rich, and the weak by the strong violates our common humanity and denies to large segments of society the blessings of life, liberty and happiness. We recognize a moral obligation to strive for a more prudent and more equitable sharing of the resources of the earth in order to ameliorate poverty, hunger and disease.

WE AFFIRM that the resources of nature are sufficient to nourish and sustain all the present inhabitants of the globe and that there is an obligation on every society to distribute those resources equitably, along with a corollary obligation upon every society to assure that its population does not place upon Nature a burden heavier than it can bear.

WE AFFIRM our responsibility to help create conditions which will make for peace and security and to build more effective machinery for keeping peace among the nations. Because the insensate accumulation of nuclear, chemical and biological weapons threatens the survival of Mankind, we call for the immediate reduction and eventual elimination of these weapons under international supervision. We deplore the reliance on force to settle disputes between nation states and between rival groups within such states.

WE AFFIRM that the oceans are the common property of mankind whose dependence on their incomparable resources of nourishment and strength will, in the next century, become crucial for human survival, and that their exploitation should be so regulated as to serve the interests of the entire globe, and of future generations.

WE AFFIRM that pollution flows with the waters and flies with the winds, that it recognizes no boundary lines and penetrates all defenses, that it works irreparable damage alike to Nature and to Mankind— threatening with extinction the life of the seas, the flora and fauna of the earth, the health of the people in cities and the countryside alike—and that it can be adequately controlled only through international cooperation.

WE AFFIRM that the exploration and utilization of outer space is a matter equally important to all the nations of the globe and that no nations can be permitted to exploit or develop the potentialities of the planetary system exclusively for its own benefit.

WE AFFIRM that the economy of all nations is a seamless web, and that no one nation can any longer effectively maintain its processes of production and monetary systems without recognizing the necessity for collaborative regulation by international authorities.

WE AFFIRM that in a civilized society, the institutions of science and the arts are never at war and call upon all nations to exempt these institutions from the claims of chauvinistic nationalism and to foster the great community of learning and creativity whose benign function it is to advance civilization and the health and happiness of mankind.

WE AFFIRM that a world without law is a world without order, and we call upon all nations to strengthen and to sustain the United Nations and its specialized agencies, and other institutions of world order, and to broaden the jurisdiction of the World Court, that these may preside over a reign of law that will not only end wars but end as well the mindless violence which terrorized our society even in times of peace.

We can no longer afford to make little plans, allow ourselves to be the captives of events and forces over which we have no control, consult our fears rather than our hopes. We call upon the American people, on the threshold of the third century of their national existence, to display once again that boldness, enterprise, magnanimity and vision which enabled the founders of our Republic to bring forth a new nation and inaugurate a new era in human history. The fate of humanity hangs in the balance. Throughout the globe, hearts and hopes wait upon us. We summon all Mankind to unite to meet the great challenge.

This Declaration of Interdependence was written exclusively for the Global Interdependence Center by Henry Steel Commager, and is an integral part of thie mission of the GIC. The documents acts as a guide to the directors and membership in their commitment to constructive global interdependence. The Global Interdependence Center (GIC) is a non-profit, non-partisan organization founded in 1976 in Philadelphia by academic, business and government leaders who anticipated the accelerating interconnectedness of individual national economies. Since its inception, the purpose of the GIC has been to convene international opinion leaders to disseminate knowledge on interdependence issues and this affect policy in the areas of trade, finance and economic development, with a recent expansion into health care.

On December 10, 1948 the General Assembly of the United Nations adopted and proclaimed the Universal Declaration of Human Rights the full text of which appears in the following pages. Following this historic act the Assembly called upon all Member countries to publicize the text of the Declaration and "to cause it to be disseminated, displayed, read and expounded principally in schools and other educational institutions, without distinction based on the political status of countries or territories."

Preamble to the Universal Declaration of Human Rights

Whereas recognition of the inherent dignity and of the equal and inalienable rights of all members of the human family is the foundation of freedom, justice and peace in the world,

Whereas disregard and contempt for human rights have resulted in barbarous acts which have outraged the conscience of mankind, and the advent of a world in which human beings shall enjoy freedom of speech and belief and freedom from fear and want has been proclaimed as the highest aspiration of the common people,

Whereas it is essential, if man is not to be compelled to have recourse, as a last resort, to rebellion against tyranny and oppression, that human rights should be protected by the rule of law,

Whereas it is essential to promote the development of friendly relations between nations,

Whereas the peoples of the United Nations have in the Charter reaffirmed their faith in fundamental human rights, in the dignity and worth of the human person and in the equal rights of men and women and have determined to promote social progress and better standards of life in larger freedom,

Whereas Member States have pledged themselves to achieve, in co-operation with the United Nations, the promotion of universal respect for and observance of human rights and fundamental freedoms,

Whereas a common understanding of these rights and freedoms is of the greatest importance for the full realization of this pledge,

Now, Therefore THE GENERAL ASSEMBLY proclaims THIS UNIVERSAL DECLARATION OF HUMAN RIGHTS as a common standard of achievement for all peoples and all nations, to the end that every individual and every organ of society, keeping this Declaration constantly in mind, shall strive by teaching and education to promote respect for these rights and freedoms and by progressive measures, national and international, to secure their universal and effective recognition and observance, both among the peoples of Member States themselves and among the peoples of territories under their jurisdiction.

About the Editors

SONDRA MYERS is a consultant for international, civic and cultural projects and a senior associate of the University of Maryland's Democracy Collaborative. Myers, the editor of the *Democracy is a Discussion* handbooks and *The Democracy Reader*, speaks and writes frequently on strengthening the culture of democracy worldwide and the integration of culture into public policy in the United States. She was the director of the first annual Interdependence Day, held at the American Philosophical Society in Philadelphia on September 12, 2003.

BENJAMIN R. BARBER is the Gershon and Carol Kekst Professor of Civil Society and Distinguished University Professor at the University of Maryland, and a principal of the Democracy Collaborative. Barber's 17 books include the classic *Strong Democracy* and the international best-seller *Jihad vs. McWorld*. A frequent advisor to political and civic leaders in the US and abroad, Barber has been a regular commentator on world affairs after 9/11. He is the founder and chair of the Interdependence Project.

About the Contributors

TARIQ ADWAN is a pre-medical student at Misericordia College in Dallas, PA.

KOFI ANNAN is the Secretary-General of the United Nations and 2001 Nobel Peace Prize Laureate.

HARRY BELAFONTE is a world-renowned singer, actor, composer, author, producer and civic activist.

JOHN BRADEMAS is President Emeritus of New York University, a former U.S. Member of Congress from Indiana and past chairman of the National Endowment for Democracy.

PATRICE BRODEUR is Dean of Religious and Spiritual Life, Associate Professor of Religious Studies, and Director of the Pluralism Project at Connecticut College.

WILLIAM JEFFERSON CLINTON was the forty-second president of the United States.

LILLY DENG is a student at Perkiomen Valley High School in Collegeville, PA.

ZAMIRA DJABOROVA is a graduate student in international studies at New School University.

SHIRIN EBADI is the 2003 Nobel Peace Prize Laureate, lecturer, lawyer and advocate for the rights of children in Iran.

HOWARD GARDNER is the John H. and Elisabeth A. Hobbs Professor of Cognition and Education at the Graduate School of Education, Harvard University and author of numerous books on learning and ways of knowing.

JOSHUA GOLDSTEIN is a student at the University of Maryland.

SETH GREEN is the coordinator of Americans for Informed Democracy (www.aidemocracy.org) and a student at the Yale Law School.

GARY HART is a former U.S. Senator from Colorado, author and lecturer. He is currently senior counsel to Coudert Brothers in Denver, CO.

VÁCLAV HAVEL, the former president of the Czech Republic, is a noted playwright and poet.

THOMAS P. HUGHES is an Emeritus Professor of the History and Sociology of Science at the University of Pennsylvania. His most recent book is *Human-Built World: How to Think about Technology and Culture* (University of Chicago Press, 2004).

JOHN F. KENNEDY was the thirty-fifth president of the United States.

MARTIN LUTHER KING, JR. was a principal leader within the United States civil rights movement, orator, author, activist and 1964 Nobel Peace Prize Laureate.

CHIARA LUBICH is the Founder and President of the Focolare Movement.

MARTHA NUSSBAUM is the Ernst Freund Distinguished Service Professor of Law and Ethics at the University of Chicago.

LEOLUCA ORLANDO is President of the Sicilian Renaissance Institute, former Mayor of Palermo and former member of the Italian and European parliaments.

SAMANTHA POWER is a 2003 Pulitzer Prize-winning author and lecturer in Public Policy at the John F. Kennedy School of Government, Harvard University.

SONIA SANCHEZ is a poet, author and lecturer. She is retired Laura Carnell Professor of English and current Presidential Fellow at Temple University.

JOSEPH STIGLITZ was Chief Economist and Senior Vice-President of the World Bank from 1997-2000. In 2001, he was awarded the Nobel Prize in Economics. He is a Professor of Economics and Finance at Columbia University.

SHASHI THAROOR is Under-Secretary-General for Communications and Public Information of the United Nations and an acclaimed author of fiction and non-fiction work.

MICHAEL THURMAN is the pastor of The Dexter Avenue King Memorial Baptist Church in Montgomery, Alabama.

The Interdependence Project
CivWorld Citizens' Campaign for Democracy
The Democracy Collaborative
1228 Tawes Hall
University of Maryland
College Park, MD 20742

For further information on the project:

Visit the CivWorld website, **www.civworld.org**
and/or contact:

Sondra Myers
1025 Connecticut Avenue, NW, Suite 701
Washington, DC 20036
sondram@ix.netcom.com

or

Benjamin R. Barber
The Democracy Collaborative, New York Office
1841 Broadway, Suite 1008
New York, NY 10023
bbarber@civworld.org